Transformed by
—— the *Power* of ——
GOD

Transformed by
the *Power* of
GOD

LEARNING TO BE CLOTHED IN JESUS CHRIST

NEIL J. GILLIGAN

DESTINY IMAGE® PUBLISHERS, INC.
P.O. Box 310, Shippensburg, PA 17257-0310

"Speaking to the Purposes of God for This Generation and for the Generations to Come."

This book and all other Destiny Image, Revival Press, MercyPlace, Fresh Bread, Destiny Image Fiction, and Treasure House books are available at Christian bookstores and distributors worldwide.

For a U.S. bookstore nearest you, call 1-800-722-6774.
For more information on foreign distributors, call 717-532-3040.
Reach us on the Internet: www.destinyimage.com.

Trade Paper ISBN 978-0-7684-3258-9
Hard Cover ISBN 978-0-7684-3460-6
Large Print ISBN 978-0-7684-3461-3
Ebook ISBN 978-0-7684-9109-8

For Worldwide Distribution, Printed in the U.S.A.
1 2 3 4 5 6 7 8 9 10 11 / 13 12 11 10

DEDICATION

I dedicate this book to my mother, Norma June Gilligan, a charismatic Catholic who prayed for me and it worked. She also loved it when she could express the Kingdom of God by healing the sick or hearing words of knowledge or just listening to the Lord. Her ceiling became my floor. Thanks, Mom. I also dedicate this book to all the spiritual sons and daughters who are called to put on the Lord Jesus Christ and impact the world with His love and power. Wake up kids, it's time to get dressed! I am praying for you.

ACKNOWLEDGMENTS

I want to acknowledge and thank all of the many individuals who worked with me over the years, directly or indirectly, and contributed to the publishing of this book. Many of you will remain unnamed, like my first college English professor, who told me I wrote like I had a Rolls-Royce engine but a Volkswagen body. Hopefully, as I have aged, my writing body has had a makeover as my physical body has started to succumb to gravity. However, I do want to specifically thank all those who helped in the development of this book in all the variety of ways they gave me encouragement and assistance so I could get this book published. They are the following: Pastor Ruth Blight, Katheran Doak, Cherie Glahn, Marci Goodwin, Linda Hackett, Carol Kindt, Nancy Mar, Pastor Mary Oliver, Pastor Edison Rodriguez, Pastor Stephen Saunders, and Jeremy Smith.

I also want to thank my Lord Jesus Christ who knew me before I was in my mother's womb and set me apart to do the good works which He had prepared for me to do. Jesus has given me insights that I never dreamed I would be allowed to see, let alone write about them. I thank You, Lord Jesus, that You are teaching me and guiding me and allowing Your life to be lived through me. I do not understand this fully yet—how I have died and how Christ lives in me—but I am beginning to understand that the script of my life that I am now living is occurring only because Christ lives in me and through me. It is an awesome adventure to be able to live the life He has given me and then to be allowed to write about it. Thanks, Lord Jesus, for everything.

ENDORSEMENTS

You will discover *Transformed by the Power of God* to be a unique approach to understanding the Christian life. Do not expect to see typical interpretations of some Scriptures.

Paul L. Cox
Aslan's Place
Hesperia, CA 92345

The Lord clearly and simply gave Neil this timely message. Believers must know that our lives are not about programs and projects, but about what we wear and carry as disciples of Jesus Christ, who we are in Him, and who He is through us. We cannot occupy until His return unless we have the skills and know the authority He gave us—without a doubt—to live a victorious life. So dress up, Christian soldiers!

Carol Kindt
Pastor in home fellowship
Author, *The Life I Now Live: Steps to Intimacy*
Sequim, Washington

Transformed by the Power of God will give you a fresh perspective about who you are in the Kingdom of God. Rich in scriptural references, it will create a shift in your thinking and equip you to live out your faith in a greater experience of God's power. Confusion about the spiritual gifts has rendered much of the Christian Church culturally irrelevant for too long. Neil's book helps cut through the clutter and replace passivity with action.

Stephen Saunders
Associate Pastor, Open Heart Ministry
Bothell, Washington

I like the book! It is a delight to read. It is easy to read. It has a refreshing immediacy to it, and it has a brightness to it. And I've never read a book focused specifically on spiritual clothing. My first impulse is to endorse it with Elijah House's permission.

Mark Sandford
Spiritual Director
Elijah House, USA

CONTENTS

INTRODUCTION

Transformed by the Power of God: Learning to Be Clothed in Jesus Christ addresses the Body of Christ with the message that we live in a *kairos* time. *Kairos* is a Greek word that means the perfect moment, a specific time or season for something special to occur. I believe in this season God has planned something special to happen in and through the Body of Christ. So right now it is a *kairos* time and we must get ready. This book explains what God desires His people to wear, so when the believers are transformed by the power of God, they are simultaneously dressed in a holy spiritual garment and empowered to demonstrate the Kingdom of God wherever they go. This is the garment that God originally intended for His people to wear, so in this book I have called it *The Designer's Clothes*.

I use the term "the Designer's Clothes" to describe the garment believers are to be dressed in, based on Jesus Christ being the Creator of the heavens and the earth, as it is *"through Him all things were made..."* (John 1:3). Since Jesus Christ is the Creator, He is also the Designer. I use the term "the Designer's Clothes" to indicate they are the same clothes that Jesus Christ wore when He lived on the earth. This is the garment that God wants all believers to wear in this season. When we put on the Designer's clothes, we are putting on the Lord Jesus Christ, and we are submitting to the Holy Spirit and allowing Him to transform us by the power of God. When I use the term "the Designer's Clothes" I am implying that the person wearing them is allowing the Holy Spirit to continue the transformation process of changing into the likeness of Jesus Christ.

Over the last few years, the Holy Spirit has enrolled me in the school of the Holy Spirit, and He has taught me that as I was being transformed by the power of God, I was also being clothed in the Holy Spirit Himself—clothed in the light of God, in the fire of God, and in the glory of God. I will share some of my own personal testimony in Chapters Three and Four about how I was being dressed by the Holy Spirit, but I want to make it clear that this is not just for me to tell my testimony. No, this message is for the whole Body of Christ to be transformed by the power of God and clothed in the Holy Spirit. This transformation empowers us to move out into the world and demonstrate that Jesus Christ truly reigns as the Son of God, for He is the King of kings and the Lord of lords.

In this book I will explain my personal journey—how I was led by the Holy Spirit to be clothed. Then I will look at the Scriptures and identify the direct and indirect references to being clothed. This is particularly linked to the Lord's desire for His followers to be transformed into His likeness, as being clothed in the Spirit is part of the process of being transformed (see 2 Cor. 3:18). Finally, I look at the prophetic end-time parables and highlight the significance that they speak about believers being clothed.

I mention in Chapter Sixteen that if we happen to be the last generation who lives upon the earth, then we have an obligation to be clothed in the Spirit's presence. The reference in these parables to the end of the age means that the Father in Heaven wants as many of the people who are living during this time to be saved as possible. Our duty, if we are that last generation to live upon the earth, is to save them, since that is why the Lord has us alive at this time. To save them in the final harvest is only possible when we are wearing the Designer's clothes and demonstrating the gifts of the Spirit. We do not know if we are currently in the last generation or if there will be a few more generations to come; however, the urgency that I have in my spirit is to get this message out—to be clothed—as I have the feeling that if we are not in the last generation alive today, that generation will be alive very soon. So this book, *Transformed by the Power of God*, is encouraging the believers who are alive today to put on the Designer's Clothes. We must be transformed by God's power and put on the Lord Jesus Christ now so the next generation will have models to emulate. They will then want to wear the Designer's clothes. This generation is alive to begin to build the momentum of believers being clothed, so the next generation will be able to catch the baton and take off from where we leave off.

A few months ago, I had finished my workout at the fitness club where I train, and I went to the grocery store to buy some bottled water. I was tired and I kind of slumped along, but as I approached the aisle I was to go down to get the water, I noticed a middle-aged woman standing by her shopping cart. All of a sudden, there was a brilliant flash of white light in front of her, and then that flash just disappeared. I walked past her and got my water, thinking, "Lord, what was that about?" When I turned around to go to the cashier, she was still standing there, and I had the impression that she was shining her light before her because she was a Christian.

I felt compelled to share with her what I saw, so I said, "Hi, I believe you are a Christian, and the reason why I say that is because when I walked past you, I saw a very bright light flash. Do remember Jesus told us we were to shine our light before men? Well, I think the Lord is encouraging you, because you are shining your light." She acknowledged that she was a Christian and thanked me for the encouragement I had given her, and then I went to pay for my water.

This lady looked a bit stunned, as if she did not really realize that she had a light. She may be typical of many Christians who do not really know that we have a light to shine. But if we are true believers, then we have a literal light that shines in the spiritual realm when we have received Jesus Christ as our Lord and Savior. Because of that, He gave us the gift of eternal life, symbolized by the lamp in our spirit (see Matt. 5:14-16). The light is not figurative—it is a literal light. What is more important is that we not only have a light to shine, but we are also required to have a quantity of oil so we can shine our light brightly. That is what this book is about. I want to encourage you, like I did that lady, to shine your light brightly—only I am urging you to be filled to overflowing with the Holy Spirit until you are transformed by the power of God and are clothed in the Spirit of God, putting on the Designer's clothes.

Transformed by the Power of God is going to encourage you to become clothed. But I will also share with you what I believe is the Father in Heaven's heart for His followers—His children. That is for us to understand the Scriptures, especially the Scriptures about the end times. In the end times, we are told that the love of most will grow cold, but the Father wants His children to express His love in the world around us (see Matt. 24:12). In this season, we need to not only be filled up, but also receive any inner healing we require, so that when the love grows cold, we can contrast that coldness with a full, healthy, whole heart of the Father's love. That way we can represent the Father in Heaven and express His love to the people around us.

Being clothed will also allow you to express the Father's love with healing, casting out demons, and prophetic encouragements, so part of this season is to learn to access those gifts of the Spirit and to practice those gifts. You are being invited to be one of God's followers who will represent Him in the world at this time. This message is for the whole Body of Christ to be clothed in the Holy Spirit, which will transform us and enable us to move out into the world and demonstrate that Jesus Christ truly reigns as the Son of God, for He is the King of kings and the Lord of lords.

As part of the next book I am writing—*Surprisingly Supernatural: A Practical Guide to Releasing the Gifts of the Spirit*—I have uploaded a number of videos onto the website "www.transformedbythepowerofgod. com" that are mentioned in Chapter Ten to help illustrate the point about impartation that I discuss in that chapter.

The theme of this book is to be continually filled by the Holy Spirit until you are clothed in Jesus Christ. That's it! But being filled by the Holy Spirit and clothed in Jesus Christ is really all about intimacy. When we are in His presence we can commune with Him and talk with Him, and through that relationship with Jesus we become like Him. We are transformed by spending time with Jesus and receiving His Spirit, so our love and our desire to obey Him becomes our focus. When those heart changes take place, we are in the right place for the gifts of the Spirit to flow from us. Without that focus, we could lapse into idolatry—wanting the gifts so badly. We are told that some who operate in the gifts of the Spirit with prophecy and miracles are cast away from the Lord (see Matt. 7:22-23). I want to encourage the reader to pursue your relationship with the Lord, since out of that relationship with the Lord Jesus the gifts and the fruit will flow abundantly through you as you are transformed into His likeness.

I want to encourage you to embrace being filled by the Holy Spirit and clothed in Jesus Christ; that is the start of walking out your birthright. All the things I share in this book are experiences I have encountered because the Holy Spirit was teaching me, not because I am a special saint, but only because I was hungry for God. The revelations I share with the reader are from the insights the Holy Spirit gave me, not because I have my own intelligence or insights, but because the Holy Spirit is with me and is teaching me and I am willing to listen and learn. In Zechariah, the prophet says, *"This is the word of the Lord to Zerubbabel: 'Not by might, nor by power, but by My Spirit,' says the Lord Almighty"* (Zech. 4:6). We then read in Haggai that the Lord stirred up the spirit within Zerubbabel, causing him to commence the rebuilding of the temple in Jerusalem (see Hag. 1:1-13; 2:4-5). Apparently Zerubbabel got the message, and he started the temple reconstruction. It is only by the Lord's Spirit that we can do what we are called to do. I got the message too, and I hope you will also see the crucial importance of being filled by the Holy Spirit.

Finally, the ideas I share with you in this book are in the spirit of humility. I am not trying to be pedantic in my presentation, but I am trying to be persuasive and curious. I am in awe of our heavenly Father and our Lord Jesus Christ, and I count it such a blessing to be born at this time and to be called to receive the Kingdom of God like a little child. So be curious and have wonder with me, and join me in the pursuit of God and His Kingdom.

PART I

~

THE HOLY SPIRIT'S TEACHING

In Part I, I explain how the Holy Spirit enrolled me in His school. The Holy Spirit began to lead me, teach me, and speak to me to abide in Jesus. Once I learned to abide in Jesus and have Jesus abide in me, my life was never the same. I was transformed and I had Jesus with me all the time via His Holy Spirit.

CHAPTER 1

"THE DESIGNER'S CLOTHES" OR DESIGNER CLOTHES?

*But everything exposed by the light becomes visible, for it is light that
makes everything visible. This is why it is said, "Wake up, O sleeper,
rise from the dead, and Christ will shine on you." Be very careful, then,
how you live—not as unwise but as wise, making the most of every
opportunity, because the days are evil. Therefore do not be foolish, but
understand what the Lord's will is. Do not get drunk on wine, which
leads to debauchery. Instead, be filled with the Spirit* (Ephesians
5:13-18).

If you look around the shopping malls in any city in the world, you
will see trendy designer clothes almost everywhere. Have you observed
that? Ralph Lauren, Guess, Gucci, Calvin Klein, Prada, and the list goes
on. So what is really going on with the push to wear designer clothes?
Do our tastes get dictated by designers who say what is trendy or not?
What is style? What color, length, and fabrics are we told to wear? Do
they dictate what we wear? Is this healthy? How about from a Christian

perspective? Should we really be wearing clothes because designers tell us to wear them? Are we acculturated into that mindset so much that we do not know what we should actually be wearing as Christians? Are fashion designer clothes a distraction? If so, what do they distract us from?

Well, the advertising people try to capture the youth and teen markets and indoctrinate them into buying and wearing the latest fashion trends that they have spun out. I believe that most people are influenced in their buying habits by these external powers, and they do not really exercise their free will when they buy designer clothes.

I failed to exercise my own free will recently when I unconsciously bought a new pair of designer eyeglasses. I liked their look. But when I got them home, my heart raced a little when I saw the designer's name was Prada. I immediately remembered the movie, *The Devil Wears Prada*. What had pulled on me to make the decision to buy those frames? Was I influenced by the devil in buying those eyeglasses?

Now, I am partially joking here, but also partially serious. I wonder if we need to reflect on what we wear as Christians. Is it possible that God really intended for human beings to be clothed in something He made? I am not saying we should wear Amish outfits or be ultra-conservative. I like many of the designs, with their colors, textures, patterns, and the creativity involved in designer fashions. However, having tried on the Designer's clothes, I can now tell you that I like the clothes God intended to clothe me in much more than I like any of the designer clothes I have purchased in fashion malls. I believe that most Christians are unaware of the clothes God has made for us.

I was unaware of this until a short time ago, but now I know that they are the most beautiful, the most wonderful, and the most important garments anyone could possibly put on. But before I put God's clothes on, I had to search the Scriptures in order to understand what I was being clothed in.

~

Discussion Questions

1. Take a moment and think about how you make your decisions to buy clothes.

   * Do you have a set wardrobe?

   * Do you ever make changes to your wardrobe? If so, how do you make those decisions?

2. Have you ever thought Christians should be distinctive dressers?

   * If so, how would that distinction appear?

   * Do you ever feel you are influenced by cultural values that do not represent your spiritual beliefs in how you dress? What do you see as acceptable?

3. Have you ever thought about or felt how being made in the image of God and being clothed with power from on high makes a difference in how a believer is seen both in the natural realm and in the spiritual realm? (See Genesis 1:27 and Luke 24:49.)

   * Reflect on the verses above and discuss the possibilities of what God could have given to those who believe.

CHAPTER 2

My Questions About Scripture

A large crowd followed and pressed in around Him. And a woman was there who had been subject to bleeding for twelve years. She had suffered a great deal under the care of many doctors and had spent all she had, yet instead of getting better she grew worse. When she heard about Jesus, she came up behind Him in the crowd and touched His cloak, because she thought, "If I just touch His clothes, I will be healed." Immediately her bleeding stopped and she felt in her body that she was freed from her suffering. At once Jesus realized that power had gone out from Him... (Mark 5:24-30).

People brought the sick into the streets and laid them on beds and mats so that at least Peter's shadow might fall on some of them as he passed by (Acts 5:15).

God did extraordinary miracles through Paul, so that even handkerchiefs and aprons that had touched him were taken to the sick, and their illnesses were cured and the evil spirits left them (Acts 19:11-12).

Have you ever read a section of Scripture and not really understood what it meant, so you just skimmed over it in kind of a daze? Well, I admit that has happened to me. I would read straight through many verses in a daze. I did this until the Holy Spirit began to teach me about the deeper truths in some well-known verses of Scripture. The first symptom that changed for me was that instead of just passing over the verse and going on, I began to be bothered in my heart and my mind about the verse I was reading. I recognized that I really did not understand what that Scripture was talking about. This bothered me, since I had graduated in 2003 from Regent College, an internationally recognized graduate school, with a Master of Christian Studies degree. It seemed as though I hardly knew anything about the Scriptures that speak of the Holy Spirit filling believers until the Holy Spirit led me through those Scriptures and guided me to ponder and meditate on them.

I was reading the gospel of John where Jesus said, *"On that day you will realize that I am in my Father, and you are in Me, and I am in you"* (John 14:20). I already understood that Jesus' Spirit was in me, but I wondered, "How am I in Him? How is Jesus in His Father?" Then I read, *"Remain in Me, and I will remain in you…"* (John 15:4). The King James Version uses the term "abide." How do you abide? Well, "abide" was the word that the Holy Spirit began whispering into my spirit again and again during this season—abide, abide, abide. "How am I to remain or abide in Jesus?" I asked myself. The Bible dictionary says that to remain means "to reside or to live in, inhabit or dwell," and abide also means to dwell (see John 15:4-5).[1] I had assumed that this was only figurative language, not a reality.

They Were Filled

The Holy Spirit led me to read a number of Scriptures in succession. In John 20, Jesus told the disciples, *"'Peace be with you! As the Father sent*

Me, I am sending you.' And with that He breathed on them and said, 'Receive the Holy Spirit'" (John 20:21-22). I had never really understood that the disciples had received the Holy Spirit before Pentecost, but the Spirit was beginning to teach me about this from the Scriptures.

Then I turned to the day of Pentecost in Acts and saw that, *"All of them were filled with the Holy Spirit and began to speak in other tongues as the Spirit enabled them"* (Acts 2:4). I observed that in this verse they were filled, and I realized that it was once again the Holy Spirit who enabled them.

I turned to Acts 4 and read, *"Then Peter, filled with the Holy Spirit…"* (Acts 4:8). This is where I sensed that the Holy Spirit was alerting me to a theme by showing me that Peter was constantly filled with the Spirit. I then continued to read that after prayer, *"… They were all filled with the Holy Spirit and spoke the word of God boldly"* (Acts 4:31). Again, the disciples were empowered by the Holy Spirit, and He enabled them to speak boldly.

Then I turned to Acts 5, which tells us about Peter's shadow: *"People brought the sick into the streets and laid them on beds and mats so that at least Peter's shadow might fall on some of them as he passed by"* (Acts 5:15). Peter was in the group of disciples who had at least three or more successive fillings of the Holy Spirit as seen in Scripture. It was obvious that he was now filled to overflowing with the Holy Spirit. The overflow of the Holy Spirit made a shadow around Peter that displayed the healing and deliverance power of the Holy Spirit.

Paul had a similar manifestation to Peter's:

> *God did extraordinary miracles through Paul, so that even handkerchiefs and aprons that had touched him were taken to the sick, and their illnesses were cured and the evil spirits left them* (Acts 19:11-12).

If the pieces of clothing around his body carried the Holy Spirit's power, then Paul's body also must have been overflowing with the Holy Spirit's power. I realized, "Paul had a shadow like Peter's."

Peter and Paul both appeared to be overflowing with the Holy Spirit. I was intrigued and wondered, "Is this possible for me?" I pondered, "Was anyone else manifesting the Holy Spirit like this?" Then I thought about the story of the woman with the blood issue who thought, *"If I just touch His clothes, I will be healed"* (Mark 5:28). She touched the tassels on Jesus' garment and she was immediately healed, and *"Jesus realized that **power had gone out from Him**..."* (Mark 5:30). Once again, I saw a connection to this theme, for Jesus had also exuded power from around His body. So since Peter, Paul, and Jesus had similar manifestations of something like a shadow that exudes the Holy Spirit's power out from their bodies, I thought, "Maybe all believers are entitled to this same manifestation!" This meant that I would be entitled to it as well. Excitement began to well up within my spirit.

I realized that the practice of being filled completely with the Holy Spirit had been suppressed in the majority of the Christian churches. However, the theme of being filled by the Spirit is found in every chapter in the letter to the Ephesians:

- Ephesians 1 says Jesus Christ is *"... the fullness of Him who fills everything in every way"* (Eph. 1:23).

- Ephesians 2 says that in Jesus Christ we are *"being built together to become a dwelling in which God lives by His Spirit"* (Eph. 2:22).

- Ephesians 3 tells believers to be filled *"to the measure of all the fullness of God"* (Eph. 3:19).

- Ephesians 4 says the saints are to attain *"to the whole measure of the fullness of Christ"* (Eph. 4:13).

- Ephesians 5 says believers are to *"be filled with the Spirit"* (Eph. 5:18).

- Ephesians 6 tells believers, *"Therefore put on the full armor of God, so that... you may be able to stand your ground, and after you have done everything, to stand"* (Eph. 6:13).

The theme in Ephesians is that we need to do everything to stand our ground, and that is to be sure that we are filled with the Holy Spirit. In Ephesians 5, the verb in the phrase, *"Be filled with the Spirit,"* has the meaning in Greek "to be continually filled" (Eph. 5:18). Therefore, being continually filled by the Holy Spirit is doing everything to stand our ground, which is the meaning behind Paul's metaphor when he said to *"put on the full armor of God"* (Eph. 6:13). The Holy Spirit was really speaking to my heart as I discerned this theme in Ephesians. I knew I needed to change my ways and learn how to be continually filled by the Holy Spirit. This was not taught in graduate school, but I was taught to be filled with the Holy Spirit in the school of the Holy Spirit as the Lord wanted me to be transformed by the power of God.

Discussion Questions

1. When you read Scripture, are you aware that you pass over sections that do not make any sense to you at the time, or do you stop and ponder them, asking the Holy Spirit for insights and revelations?

   ⚫ Discuss and share the Scriptures that you tend to pass over.

2. We see from the verses in John and Acts that many fillings preceded Peter's miraculous shadow experience, and that Paul's teaching, *"Be filled with the Holy Spirit,"* actually means to be continually filled (Eph. 5:18). Discuss if these scriptural truths have been suppressed in your life or not.

   ⚫ Discuss any misconceptions that you were taught about being filled with the Spirit.

   ⚫ Confess any lies that have kept you from being continually filled with the Holy Spirit. Lies may be, "I am saved; that's all I need to live the Christian life," or, "I got the Holy Spirit when I first believed; I don't need any more of the Holy Spirit."

   ⚫ You may want to pray a prayer of repentance like the following one:

   Heavenly Father, I confess that I have been deceived by the lies of the enemy. I was blinded to see that I was deprived in my life as a Christian by not being continually filled with the Holy Spirit. As a result I have not been able to testify about Jesus Christ as You would have wanted me to. Please forgive me.

I repent and I ask for Your grace to guide me to be disciplined in pursuing being filled by the Holy Spirit on a daily basis. I thank You for this revelation and the grace You will give me that I will now learn to walk through life as the man or the woman of God You intended for me to be. I thank You that I will do all of the works You planned in advance for me to do, by Your grace. In Jesus' name, Amen.

3. Since Jesus, Peter, and Paul all appeared to have miraculous shadows or clothing around their bodies, do you think you also can have that manifestation of the Holy Spirit?

4. Discuss what you need to do to have a shadow like Peter's, Paul's or Jesus'.

ENDNOTE

1. James Strong, *The Exhaustive Concordance of The Bible: Showing Every Word of the Text of the Common English Version of the Canonical Books* (Nashville, TN: Abingdon, 1980). (G3306): "μένω menō men'-o"

CHAPTER 3

LEARNING TO BE FILLED

As Jesus was coming up out of the water, He saw Heaven being torn open and the Spirit descending on Him like a dove. And a voice came from Heaven: "You are My Son, whom I love; with You I am well pleased" (Mark 1:10-11).

... Do not leave Jerusalem, but wait for the gift My Father promised, which you have heard Me speak about. For John baptized with water, but in a few days you will be baptized with the Holy Spirit (Acts 1:4-5).

We proclaim Him, admonishing and teaching everyone with all wisdom, so that we may present everyone perfect in Christ. To this end I labor, struggling with all His energy, which so powerfully works in me (Colossians 1:28-29).

I read about some of the leading Christian healing evangelists like Benny Hinn and Reinhard Bonke, and I learned from them that the key was to be filled with the Holy Spirit. These evangelists showed that they were immersed in the Holy Spirit's anointing, and from that immersion they were able to proclaim the Gospel of Jesus Christ. They participated in a worldwide campaign of miracles, healings, deliverances, and prophetic words. When I read about that, the thought came to me that maybe I can do that too.[1]

So I began to ask the Holy Spirit to fill me, and I learned to "soak" in the Holy Spirit's presence. I did this for several hours a day. (See Appendix A: Soaking—this is an outline of how to soak and to be filled with the Holy Spirit.) After several months of soaking, I was not launched into a worldwide campaign, but I had begun to understand that I was called into my birthright. Some prophets told me I would be a trainer and equipper for God's army and a prophet to the nations. For some reason, I believed those prophetic words and began to decree them back to God. By the year's end, I was invited to run a healing room ministry. The Lord responded to my faith and launched me into the spiritual realm of healings, miracles, and prophetic words that came to pass right before my eyes.

A SPIRIT TOUCH

The first time I set my heart to engage with God by asking the Holy Spirit to come and fill me, I had a beautiful experience with God. Suddenly, I felt the Holy Spirit land on my open palms like a bird alighting on my hand. I thought, "Wow, that's cool." And then I wondered, "Is this the dove of the Holy Spirit?" (See Mark 1:10.) I then had a rush of excitement when I realized that the God who created the whole universe was actually touching me and connecting with me. Then my heart burst open in response to the love I received from the Father and the Son. Deep passionate love flowed out from my heart and tears poured out of my eyes as I expressed how much I loved Jesus and how much I desired to be with my God. This was a breakthrough experience, but the intensity of the emotional response lasted for only a couple of days.

When I asked the Holy Spirit to fill me, I usually felt the Holy Spirit come and fill me through my hands, and also through the bottoms of my feet. I felt the power come in more dominantly on the left side of my body, which some describe as the personal side or the heart's side. The right side is the social side of the body that we use to greet other people by shaking hands with them. The Holy Spirit would come in through my hand, go up my forearm to my bicep and triceps, into my shoulder, and then it appeared to move into my torso. The Holy Spirit would also come up from the soles of my feet into my leg, through my calf, up my hamstrings and thigh, and go into my hip girdle. When this first happened, I was amazed at the experience. I realized I was actually being filled! I had never really understood it when I had read in Scripture that I was to be literally and abundantly filled with the Spirit. It was as if I had thought that being filled was like taking one of those little Dixie cups and drinking it. I thought that was being filled! But no! God wanted me to understand that I was not to take the little cup, but that I had to guzzle the whole bottle down each and every day to be filled. This was the new wine Jesus talked about, and I was learning to fill my new wineskin with this new wine (see Mark 2:22).

I also felt the Holy Spirit come and touch me on my face and head. I would often feel the Spirit touch my forehead and the top of my nose. But sometimes He would touch my cheek and my lips. I would feel the movement of the Holy Spirit on my cheek, and I would track its direction. It was such an intimate touch, like the touch a lover would make on your cheek. I felt as if Jesus was going to give me a kiss. So I followed the movement of the anointing as it moved down my cheek, caressing it, then it would lightly tickle my chin, and then He just moved ever so briefly onto my lips. He did kiss me! I was amazed at how intimate and lovely the Lord was with me. It was far more intimate than I had ever been with the Holy Spirit before.

In the process of writing this section of the book, the Holy Spirit has come many times and given me a kiss. Being kissed by God has only happened once in a while since those initial experiences of feeling the anointing on my nose and forehead, but He helped me to be secure in my heart, knowing that He is so intimate and is so wonderful to be in relationship with.

I always soaked with the palms of my hands facing upward. After about three months of soaking for several hours a day, I went out to Starbucks for coffee with a friend. As we were talking, I happened to turn the palm of my hand up, and suddenly I felt the Holy Spirit land on it. I was a little shocked, yet I was delighted that the Holy Spirit had followed me to the coffee shop. I wondered, "Does He like Starbucks too?"

I began to think about the verse in Matthew where Jesus tells us to:

> Go and make disciples of all nations, baptizing them in the name of the Father and of the Son and of the Holy Spirit, and teaching them to obey everything I have commanded you. **And surely I will be with you always,** to the very end of the age (Matthew 28:20).

Making disciples of nations is linked to the baptism of the Holy Spirit and Jesus' promise that He would always be with us. I thought, "If the Holy Spirit keeps hanging around me and filling me, then somehow I can be used to help disciple nations." I was excited, for I sensed that I was becoming God's workmanship, created in Christ Jesus to do good works, which God prepared in advance for me to do (see Eph. 2:10). I began to wonder what those works were that God had prepared for me.

WORKING FOR THE LORD

I began to feel as if I was hurtling toward my birthright in Christ, and I was really hungry for it. I wanted to seize that birthright, so I practiced the habit of leaving the palm of my hand open toward Heaven with the intent of receiving more of God wherever I went. So when I talked and drank coffee I left my palm open, making myself available for the Holy Spirit to fill me, and He obliged me by filling me through my open hand and showing me that He was always with me. Wherever I went, whether I drove, ate a meal, or read a book, I just wanted more of God, so I left my hand open to receive more. I was hungry for Him, and I still am hungry for more of God. After several more months went by, I not only felt the Holy Spirit had filled me, but also that the flow appeared to reverse direction. He seemed to be flowing out from my hands. This experience first began when I attended some meetings at the Toronto Airport Christian Fellowship (TACF) in 2005.

When I was in the TACF Leadership School during worship, I heard the Holy Spirit whisper into my spirit, "Feel." So with my up-stretched arms, I began to feel the air around me. I began to sense that the Holy Spirit had a palpable presence—He had a viscosity. I perceived that the Holy Spirit appeared to have something like mass to His presence.

The next day I was in a prayer circle with a group of men, and each one of us had his arms around the shoulders of the guy on either side. I suddenly felt within me the emotions from the guy on my right. I sensed fear, anger, and sadness, and then I felt that the guy on my left was pulling the power of God out of my hand and into his back. I decided it was safer to talk with the guy with the back issue than to the guy with the emotional issues. So I asked him, "What is happening to you?"

He told me that the power of God was flowing down into his lower back to a place where he had an injury, and he told me that he was feeling heat from the anointing. I asked the group of guys to pray with me, and we checked his progress. On the first check, he was 50 percent better, on the second, 75 percent better, but before we could check him for a third time, he fell down to the floor under the Holy Spirit's power. This was the first fruit I had seen from having waited for several months for the Holy

Spirit to fill me. I began to enjoy the new experiences that God was allowing me to participate in.

Later that week I prayed for other people, and I was again aware of the anointing flowing through me into the people I ministered to. This was new to me, and I was delighted that the Holy Spirit had given me gifts of healing power. I also discovered He had given me the gift of discernment in my hands.

A short while later I drove to Billings, Montana, to catch Benny Hinn in his healing crusade. I wanted to learn how he operated in the healing gifts. As I drove, I kept my hand open to receive the Holy Spirit, and I began to notice that the intensity of the Holy Spirit would increase or decrease as I drove through cities. Sometimes it appeared to get stronger when I entered a town, and other times it got stronger as I exited a town. I shared my experiences about this gift of discernment with a pastor from Calgary, and I told him what happened when I drove through the city of Lethbridge, Alberta. I told him I sensed a strong anointing to the east side, but it faded toward the center of town, and then it increased as I drove to the next town to the west. He told me the church and headquarters for the Miracle Channel was on the east side, a secular college was in the center of the city, and the next town had a large, active, Spirit-filled church in it. His feedback helped me to understand that the Lord had equipped me with discernment in my hands for open heavens. When the anointing was more intense in my hand it indicated that there was an open heaven; with the open heavens more anointing from the Holy Spirit could get through and fill me. The lower intensity indicated that the heaven was somehow blocked. (See Daniel 10:12-14; Mark 6:1-5.)

I began to feel more of the power of God being released from my fingers. I gradually realized that this power was for healing, deliverance, and impartation. Healings were beginning to be more consistent, and I was noticing that my hands were getting hotter when I prayed for people. I would put my hands on people's sore and tight muscles and command the pain and tension to go in Jesus' name. Almost immediately, I would feel the muscles begin to relax and get softer. I realized I was beginning to operate in both the power and authority of God.

Sometimes I would just sit in a coffee shop and feel the power of God coming out of my fingers. I began to experiment, and I noticed that when I put my fingers together, I felt that the intensity of the power would increase. Then I wondered, "Is this the light of God, the fire of God, or what? Can this light go through anything?" So I put my fingers on either side of my porcelain coffee mug, and I felt that the intensity of the power between my fingers had intensified—"Wow, it went right through the coffee mug!" I began to ask my waiters to put their fingers on the other side of the coffee mug, while I placed my fingers on the opposite side. I would ask, "Do you feel anything?"

The waiter would usually say, "Yes, I feel vibrations," or, "I feel heat," or, "I feel energy." I estimate that about 70 percent of the people felt something; however, some felt nothing at all.

When the people who felt something in their own hands told me they were feeling something, it gave me the opportunity to witness to them about Jesus Christ. I would tell them that the power they felt was the power of Jesus' Holy Spirit. As a result, several people received Jesus Christ as their Savior due to this anointing experience.

I meditated on the coffee mug experience for a few weeks and wondered, "Since the light of God went through the porcelain of a coffee mug, could it also go through bone, skin, muscles, and tendons? If a demon was hiding in a person, would the light cut right into it? Would the demon think, 'Oh no, Jesus is here! Yikes! Let's go!'" I was bemused and excited that the school of the Holy Spirit was really giving me insights that I had never learned anywhere else.

I asked a Muslim cashier at a coffee shop to feel how cold my hand was. She touched it and confirmed that it was cold. Then I asked her to point her fingers toward mine and tell me what she felt. She replied, "I feel heat."

So I asked, "How do you get heat from cold hands?" She looked puzzled. Then I shared, "I pray for the sick in Jesus' name and they get healed. The heat you felt was the power of Jesus Christ's Spirit." She just looked at me, and then turned to go back to her work. The wonderful thing about operating through the Holy Spirit's power was that this woman could not deny that she felt heat from a cold hand. She had a supernatural experience. I have prayed for her occasionally, asking God to bless her and to reveal Jesus to her in dreams and in other ways.

SENSING THE SPIRIT

Habakkuk talks about God and says:

> *His splendor was like the sunrise; rays flashed from His hand, where His power was hidden* (Habakkuk 3:4).

This description of God was seen by the prophet Habakkuk in a vision. Paul writes that, *"For those God foreknew He also predestined to be conformed to the likeness of His Son…"* (Romans 8:29). So as we are conformed to the likeness of Christ through the work of the Holy Spirit in us, we begin to receive manifestations of Jesus Christ's character, power, body, mind, emotions, and clothing. As Paul said, God reveals *"His Son in me"* (Gal. 1:16). I realized God had given me a manifestation like the rays that flashed from God's hands as seen by Habakkuk in the vision. It is such a blessing and honor and so humbling to know that I am being transformed into the likeness of Christ through the Holy Spirit filling me, allowing me to see and hear the confirmations of my transformation and see that they represent the manifestation of Jesus Christ in my life.

I want to clarify that the ability I have been given to feel the Holy Spirit on and in my body is a gift from God. I am not more holy or honorable than anyone else who does not feel this. But I am accountable to God to use this ability for His glory and for the edification of His Body. Very possibly, God has given me this gift of feeling the anointing in order to help other people get an idea of how the Holy Spirit works and how He reveals Himself through our physical senses.[2]

Some people have a prejudice against the physical senses, but in Hebrews we read, *"But solid food is for the mature, who by constant use have trained themselves to **distinguish** good from evil"* (Heb. 5:14). The New International Version uses the English word "distinguish," but the King James Version uses "discern" to translate the Greek word: *diakrisis. Diakrisis* means "to *discriminate,* discern, doubt, judge, etc."[3]

In First Kings 3:9 we are told that Solomon also wanted to distinguish between good and evil. The English word "discern" or "distinguish" is translated from the Hebrew word *bene. Bene* means "feel, perceive, view, and also to *separate* mentally or *distinguish, understand,* attend, consider, discern, etc."[4] *Bene* is also the Hebrew word used when Job says:

*Is there wickedness on my lips? Can my mouth not **discern** malice?* (Job 6:30)

We can see from the definition of the Hebrew word *bene* that both Solomon's and Job's discernments imply the use of the physical senses—feeling, perceiving, viewing, seeing, or tasting—to discern good from evil. Some scholars believe that the most accurate way to translate discern for these three verses is by using the five physical senses.

God made Adam and Eve, and God said it *"was very good"* (Gen. 1:31). God's approval included the approval of the physical senses that He gave to all people to help us discern good from evil. If believers could believe that God has given us our physical senses to aid in discernment of good from evil, then we would be more open to the ways that God communicates with us.

The Lord reinforced this understanding for me when I was writing this section. He taught me some things when I ministered in my church in the evening. I was helping someone by casting out a demon when I suddenly smelled a foul smell waft past my nose, and I knew it was a foul spirit leaving. God had given me the discernment in my nose that informed me that the evil spirit had left. When I was working with another person, I discerned with my hand an ungodly spiritual presence that was in front of that person. Both of these acts of discernment were brought to my physical senses of smell and touch.

My senses have opened up more because I believe that God wants to communicate that way as well. One spiritual principle is that we get whatever we believe in. Some people will just have to accept this understanding by faith, since they do not now feel or see what the Holy Spirit is doing. However, they can develop their spiritual gifts with faith, training, and practice. Other people may see and feel spiritual revelations on a much deeper level than what I have shared. Regardless of how much or how little revelation a person is aware of, it does not refute the main point that we all need to be filled regularly by the Holy Spirit. He opens up the spiritual realms to us whether we feel it, see it, or do not feel or see it at all. We must regularly ask with faith to be filled by the Holy Spirit.

~

Discussion Questions

1. Read Zechariah 4:1-7 and discuss this phrase: *"'Not by might nor by power, but by my Spirit,' says the Lord Almighty"* (Zech. 4:6).

   ❧ Reflect on this verse and determine if you actually believe it. Do you think that good will happen only through the Spirit pouring into us, or do you think that your own human efforts will avail much?

2. Paul says, *"And just as we have borne the likeness of the earthly man, so shall we bear the likeness of the Man from Heaven"* (1 Cor. 15:49).

   ❧ Discuss what the likenesses of the heavenly man may look like. Do you look like that at all?

   ❧ How do you currently walk in the likeness of Christ?

   ❧ Dream about the likenesses of Christ that you would like to bear. Tell God in prayer what your desire is.

3. Do you feel the presence of the Holy Spirit on your body?

   ❧ If not, pray and ask the Father to awaken your physical senses to the Holy Spirit.

   ❧ Pray Romans 6:13 over yourself, offering the parts of your body as instruments of righteousness.

   Here is a Prayer Sample from Romans 6:13 that you might want to pray:

   Father in Heaven, Your Word says I am to offer myself to You my God, as one who has been brought from death to life; and so I now offer the parts of my body to You as instruments of righteousness.

So I give You my eyes as instruments of righteousness, so that when I look through them I see what You want me to see.

I give You my ears as instruments of righteousness to hear what You want me to hear.

I give You my nose as an instrument of righteousness to smell what You want me to smell.

I give You my mouth as an instrument of righteousness to taste what You want me to taste.

I give You my hands as instruments of righteousness to feel what You want me to feel and touch what You want me to touch.

I give You my whole body as an instrument of righteousness that You might take possession of it for Your Kingdom purposes.

I ask this all in Jesus' name, Amen.

ENDNOTES

1. Todd Bentley, *Journey into the Miraculous* (Pineville, NC: Fresh Fire, 2003), 43-247. (Todd Bentley's website gives more information about his ministry at www.freshfire.ca).

2. Prophet Bob Jones said in 2002 that the Lord was going to release the five senses to the body for spiritual discernment. The discerning heart that Solomon asked the Lord for in Second Chronicles has to do with the consciousness of a person, which includes being physically conscious of the five senses.

3. Strong, *The Exhaustive Concordance* (G1223): "διάκρισις diakrisis dee-ak'-ree-sis"

4. Ibid., (H995): "bîyn or bene"

CHAPTER 4

MORE MANIFESTATIONS OF JESUS

And these signs will accompany those who believe: In My name they will drive out demons; they will speak in new tongues; they will pick up snakes with their hands; and when they drink deadly poison, it will not hurt them at all; they will place their hands on the sick people and they will get well (Mark 16:17-18).

God came from Teman, the Holy One from Mount Paran. Selah. His glory covered the heavens and His praise filled the earth. His splendor was like the sunrise; rays flashed from His hand, where His power was hidden (Habakkuk 3:3-4).

But if I drive out demons by the finger of God, then the Kingdom of God has come to you (Luke 11:20).

In February of 2006, I was asked to preach at the *Full Gospel* church in Calgary on "Healing," since I was the healing rooms' associate director and trainer. That night I prophesied that God would allow me to see miracles right before my eyes in the coming year. God did not wait until the year ended to fulfill this prophecy. I had my first opportunity in the spring of 2006 to travel with Randy Clark's Global Awakening ministry to Brazil; subsequently, I have gone there several more times to minister.[1] On that first trip to Brazil I prayed in Jesus' name and saw miracles right before my eyes—blind eyes were opened, a boy who had a deaf and dumb spirit had it cast out so he could hear and speak, a woman in a wheelchair who had not walked for a year was healed and got up and walked, a woman with Parkinson's disease who was shaking stopped shaking and smiled, and many other people received prophetic words of encouragement that God shared through me.

Participating in these miracles was new to me, but since I had meditated on Mark 16, believed it, and internalized what Jesus had said—that believers would drive out demons and lay hands on the sick and they would recover when it was done in His name—I was able to see them manifest right before my eyes (see Mark 16:17-18). I saw Jesus backing up His Word by performing those miracles and deliverances through me. By internalizing that Scripture and believing it in my heart, I began to operate at a new level of faith in Jesus, and also in a new level of self-identity. I began to decree Scriptures on healing and my own identity in Christ during my daily devotionals. Then I began to walk them out in my life everywhere I went, whether I was in Brazil, in the healing rooms, or in restaurants in North America.

IMPARTATION

On one trip, I roomed with a Pastor Dale Foote from Kuna, Idaho. Dale told me that he had prayed for his roommate for this trip. I laughed and thought he didn't know who he was getting, having me for his roommate. But it turned out we hit it off well. We empathized with one another, since not many people in our relational circles were pressing into the deeper things of God. I shared with Dale about the power of God in my fingers, and I imparted to him this gift of the Holy Spirit that I had received. He also felt the Holy Spirit in his hands, and a short time later I noticed that he was pointing his fingers toward others like I had. He confirmed that he, too, felt the intensity of the Holy Spirit's power in his hands. This was a relief for me as sometimes I thought I was going a little crazy, because no one else I knew had experienced these manifestations of the Holy Spirit. I ended up being glad that he had prayed for his room-mate and got me.

When we were at the crusade in Fortaleza, Brazil, Randy Clark shared a vision that someone had told him that night. In the vision, he was seen "pointing his extended hand toward the crowd of people and a white light was flowing out" of his hands. When the light touched people, they were either healed or were freed of demons.

I listened to this vision and wondered, "Could this be what God is in-viting me into—this manifestation of healing light flowing out of me into other people, healing them, and setting them free from demons?"[2]

A few minutes later, it was announced, "We need any team members who can help in the deliverance tent to go to that tent now."

I thought, "I think I can help since I have done a little deliverance be-fore, and while I am helping I could learn more about it." So I went to the deliverance tent. A Brazilian leader was in front of the group of about fifty people, leading them in renunciation prayers. He paced back and forth on the platform, chanting deliverance prayers in Portuguese, and the people who were standing in front of him were echoing his words. After a few min-utes of watching, a girl fell to the ground right in front of me. I bent down to see if she was all right, and an interpreter came over and said, "We should get her into a chair." I helped her up and put her in the chair, and suddenly, I was drafted into the role of doing the deliverance—I was not simply help-ing another person with the deliverance as I had expected, no. Amazingly,

I was supposed to do it now. God was getting His way once again, as I continued my education in the school of the Holy Spirit.

As I conducted the interview, I found a few of the paths that opened her up to the demonic; we had her confess her sin, and then we cast out a few demons. We began to discuss her relationship with her father, and then she said, "My stomach is now painful, and there is something moving inside of it." I asked her to pray to forgive her father, but she got stuck on the word "forgive." She could only stutter, but she could not speak it out.

Since I felt that the anointing in my hands was really strong, I pointed my fingers to her stomach and said, "I command all ungodly spirits, in Jesus' name, to come up and out on the breath now." Then I pointed my fingertips toward her stomach from a distance of about ten centimeters, and I moved them slowly upwards from her stomach to her throat. As I approached the throat, she quickly got up and ran to the window and threw up outside through the window. As she was hanging her head out of the window, I went behind her and pointed my fingers with the power of God coming out of them toward her lower back and said, "I command all evil spirits to come up and out of her by the finger of God" (see Luke 11:20). So as I moved my fingers up from her lower back to her upper back, she would undulate and throw up again, releasing even more demons that were in her.

THE FINGER OF GOD

The NET Bible says that the "finger of God" text in Luke 11:20 is a figurative reference to Exodus 8, where Pharaoh is told by the magicians, *"'This is the finger of God.' But Pharaoh's heart was hard and he would not listen..."* (Exod. 8:19).[3] However, from my experience I do not think Luke 11:20 is a figurative reference. I believe it ties into the reference in Habakkuk 3 that states, *"... Rays flashed from His hand, where His power was hidden"* (Hab. 3:4). Consequently, Jesus was manifesting the Father's power; through His hands the rays of God's power flashed, and as a result, Jesus cast out demons with those flashing rays from His fingers. This is why He said, *"But if I drive out demons by the finger of God, then the Kingdom of God has come to you"* (Luke 11:20). Academics who have never been filled by the Holy Spirit give their own interpretations, which are their best guesses on the Scriptures, but frequently they filter out some of the literal spiritual meanings that Jesus had intended.

As I mentioned earlier, I was not very experienced in deliverance, and now I know that I should have commanded the demons not to make a scene. I should have forbid them to cause her to throw up, instead commanding them to come up and out on the breath without any manifestations. However, I did not do that, but what I did do was gain more experience in the school of the Holy Spirit. He was teaching me that the power of God flowing out of my hands could also be used for deliverance. This was another manifestation of the likeness of Christ that the Holy Spirit was working into me that ties into Luke 11:20. My experience in the school of the Holy Spirit has shown me that the power of God flows out of my fingers. So my fingers actually become "the finger of God," and as a result, demons are driven out of people. (Jodi's testimony in Appendix C is another one of the many incidences of the finger of God's manifestation that I have experienced where demons were driven out.) So that night in Fortaleza, I repeated that same action several times, and each time I reached the girl's upper back with my fingers, she would vomit and release more demons.

The events the Holy Spirit had woven together were amazing. They ranged from my coffee mug experiments to my pondering, "Could this light of God go through bone to drive out demons?" They also ranged from Dale's friendship and his sharing of his experiences with the power of God; to Randy sharing about the vision in Fortaleza that revealed the light of God flowing out of his hands to heal and deliver people; and finally, to my volunteering to help in deliverance, only to find out that God was teaching me to use His power through my fingers to cast out demons. The school of the Holy Spirit has been so much fun for me. It gives me a whole new perspective on being a Christian. Now I just want to release the Kingdom of God wherever I go.

Although this is how the Lord has equipped me to operate—having the power of God flow through my fingers—this is not a formula for every Christian to operate in the same way. Other believers will be gifted with this manifestation of the Spirit, and some other believers will not have this manifestation. We each have our part to play, and when we play our part, we are not better or more anointed than those who do not function in that manifestation. I have found that the Father in Heaven responds to His children and gives them good gifts. So, if you want spiritual blessings in Christ Jesus, you can begin to ask the Father for that gifting. He is the Giver of good gifts, so if He deems it to be a good gift for you, I am sure you will receive whatever gift you ask Him for.

MIRACLE POWER

On subsequent trips to Brazil, I also had the opportunity to minister in deliverance and healing, and I saw more of God's miraculous power released through me. One boy that I prayed for had HIV, but a few days later, he testified that all his symptoms were gone; another young man with bow legs suddenly had his left leg straightened during prayer. These more dramatic healings occurred because Jesus was doing them through me. His Spirit was living in me and was birthing new and exciting healings and miracles. But it was also quite interesting that I received still other manifestations of Jesus' likeness in my life.

One Sunday, as part of the Global Awakening trip, I was asked to preach in a Brazilian church. That day I lay down on my bed to soak in God's presence, and I closed my eyes. The Spirit was quite strong that day, and when I opened my eyes it seemed as if someone else was looking out from my eyes. I asked, "Jesus, is that You?" I did not hear a response, but just a few seconds later, my normal vision returned. I do not know why this manifestation occurred, but I can tell you that I am thankful it did, for it was as if Jesus was reassuring me that He was with me—Emanuel—God with us. That revelation gave me more faith and confidence so I could move out in greater levels for healing and do His miraculous works.

On another trip to Brazil, I ministered deliverance to a man who told me that he saw an angel touch his own eyes and ears during the worship— he was a seer. After his demon was driven out, I looked into his eyes to see if there were any other demons there. The man told me afterwards, "You know, when you were looking in my eyes, I was looking in yours, and I saw that your eyes were flames of fire."

In Revelation 1, Jesus' eyes are described: *"His eyes were like blazing fire"* (Rev. 1:14). On other occasions, other prophetic people began to share this revelation with me. Antonio's testimony in Appendix C is one example. It was so encouraging to hear these spiritual insights. I mention these stories here in humility that the Lord Jesus Christ would use me and that He began to manifest Himself through me. I am both humbled and honored by this blessing. I never really understood how my transformation and my going from glory to glory would happen. These insights began to lead me to Scriptures that talk about our transformation into the likeness of Christ, and they showed me that they are not just rhetoric— they are reality. I never ever learned this before, and I am so happy to have been taken through the school of the Holy Spirit.

I mention manifestations that I have gone through to encourage the believers who are reading this to know that they, too, are called to manifest and demonstrate the Lord Jesus Christ through their own physical and spiritual being into the world around them. These manifestations are for all believers; your only requirement is to be thirsty and hungry for the Holy Spirit.

I was also made aware of some other manifestations. The first occurred in 2006 when I attended Randy Clark's healing school in Alaska. A seer told my friend Dee McKinney that when she saw me lying on the floor, soaking, her eyes were opened and she saw that I was "all on fire." Then, in November of 2007, at the Heaven Trek conference, Dr. Paul Cox spoke over me, "Fire, I sense fire," describing what was all around me.[4] Psalms says, *"He makes winds his messengers, flames of fire his servants"* (Ps. 104:4). Hebrews tells us that God is speaking of His angels when He says, *"He makes His angels winds, His servants flames of fire"* (Heb. 1:7). I wondered, "Could this description be taken further than God's angels? Could it be that God intends to cover all His servants with fire?" The Greek word for "servants" is *leitorgos* and means a public servant. Perhaps when believers are filled to overflowing with the Spirit of God and die to themselves, they actually become the Lord's public servants of fire.

In July of 2007, at the Youth Power Invasion in Sao Paulo, Brazil, I had the opportunity to pray and impart the gifts of the Spirit into one of the worship dancers. I just pointed my fingers toward her open palms. An intercessor was standing next to us, watching, and she said to me, "I see bolts of lightning coming from your fingers." Again it appears that the phrase *"rays flashed from His hand"* from Habakkuk 3:4 was confirmed by this seer's comment that this manifestation of Christ has been given to me.

I have been truly blessed to be filled with the Holy Spirit and to see the Kingdom of God explode around me. I feel as if this is what I was meant to do all my life, and now God has finally revealed it to me. As this was happening, I sensed that God was clothing me in Himself. So I began to look in the Bible for indications of this possible reality.

MANIFEST FRUIT

Galatians 5 lists the fruit of the Spirit: *"love, joy, peace, patience, kindness, goodness, faithfulness, gentleness, and self-control..."* (Gal. 5:22-23). So when we have the Holy Spirit, we are able to express these fruits in our lives. Paul also tells us to *"clothe yourselves with compassion, kindness, humility, gentleness and patience"* (Col. 3:12). So when we are clothed in the Designer's clothes, we put on both the gifts of the Spirit and the fruit of the Spirit.

I was traveling back home from a conference at Christian International in Santa Rosa Beach, Florida, in 2007, and I had arrived at 6:15 A.M. in Charlotte, North Carolina. I had to catch my next flight at 7:00 A.M., so I lay down and began to soak. After about half an hour, I got up and went to the departure gate. Two men were ahead of me, and when I got to the attendant, I just said, "May I ask you a question about my connection?"

Her eyes got bigger and she said, "Oh, thank you for being so gentle."

I responded with, "You're welcome, but why do you need to thank me?"

She said, "It's just that everyone else who came up here yelled at me, but you were so gentle."

I had no idea that I was gentle, but by soaking in the Holy Spirit, I was able to release the gentleness of the Holy Spirit as I spoke with her (see Gal. 5:22). God was expressing His love for that attendant through me. I really felt like I did nothing to be thanked for, except I yielded myself to the Holy Spirit. He worked through me what He needed in the moment—His gentleness—so He could bless that attendant through me.

More manifestations of Jesus Christ mean greater transformation into the likeness of Christ, and this includes manifestations of the gifts of the Spirit and the fruit of the Spirit. However, Scripture is clear that the manifestation of the gifts can become idolatry if they are sought outside of a relationship with the Lord:

> *Not everyone who says to Me, "Lord, Lord," will enter the King-dom of Heaven, but only he who does the will of My Father who is in Heaven. Many will say to Me on that day, "Lord, Lord, did we not prophesy in Your name, and in Your name drive out demons and perform many miracles?" Then I will tell them plainly, "I never knew you. Away from Me, you evildoers!"* (Matthew 7:21-23)

The pursuit of the gifts of the Spirit outside of a relationship with Jesus Christ and the Father is inadvisable, as you might end up in hell if you pursue them on their own. However, I believe the Lord wants inti-mate relationships with all His children, and I also believe He wants to see us transformed, which results in greater manifestations of the likeness of our Lord Jesus Christ and the gifts and the fruit of the Spirit. When we manifest an aspect of Jesus Christ, it means we have put Him on—we are clothed in Jesus Christ. But I did not understand that I was clothed in Jesus Christ until I looked at the Scriptures on this topic.

~

Discussion Questions

1   Jesus said, *"I am the vine; you are the branches. If a man remains in Me and I in him, he will bear much fruit; apart from Me you can do nothing"* (John 15:5).

   ❧ What does Jesus mean by *"Apart from Me you can do nothing?"*

   ❧ What is the fruit we bear if we remain in Jesus and He remains in us?

   ❧ Are you deceived about the fruit you bear in your life? Do you operate in your own strength?

   ❧ How much of the time are you operating in your own strength, and how much of the time are you in Christ?

2. Paul teaches about the fruit of the Spirit in Galatians 5. Do you believe that the Holy Spirit can actually give you character traits, emotional responses, and gentleness?

   ❧ Which fruit of the Spirit do you not tend to manifest?

3. Pray and ask God to fill you with His Holy Spirit and ask for any of the fruit that you are deficient in.

ENDNOTES

1. The website is www.GlobalAwakening.com.

2. Used by permission of Randy Clark.

3. NET Bible, http://net.bible.org/passage.php?passage=Luk%206:20;11:20;17:20-21#n6 (accessed February 25, 2010).

4. Dr. Paul Cox's comment can be seen on my website, www.flame-of-fire.com, under the testimony section.

PART II

~

SCRIPTURAL PERSPECTIVES

In Part II, I explore the Scripture to confirm if the reality of being clothed by the Father in heaven is really a biblical truth. And to my joy, I find that it is.

CHAPTER 5

SCRIPTURE ON BEING CLOTHED BY GOD

What is more, I consider everything a loss compared to the surpassing greatness of knowing Christ Jesus my Lord, for whose sake I have lost all things. I consider them rubbish, **that I may gain Christ and be found in Him,** *not having a righteousness of my own that comes from the law, but that which is through faith in Christ—the righteousness that comes from God and is by faith* (Philippians 3:8-9).

For those God foreknew He also predestined to be conformed to the likeness of His Son, that He might be the firstborn among many brothers (Romans 8:29).

... So let us... put on the armor of light (Romans 13:12).

Clothe yourselves with the Lord Jesus Christ... (Romans 13:14).

As God's chosen people, holy and dearly loved, clothe yourselves with compassion, kindness, humility, gentleness and patience (Colossians 3:12).

I am going to send you what My Father has promised; but stay in the city until you have been clothed with power from on high (Luke 24:49).

*... For the trumpet will sound, the dead will be raised imperishable, and we will be changed. For **the perishable must clothe itself with the imperishable, and the mortal with immortality*** (1 Corinthians 15:52-53).

Above the expanse over their heads was what looked like a throne of sapphire, and high above on the throne was a figure like that of a Man. I saw that from what appeared to be His waist up He looked like glowing metal, as if full of fire, and that from there down He looked like fire; and brilliant light surrounded Him (Ezekiel 1:26-27).

... His face shone like the sun, and His clothes became as white as the light (Matthew 17:2).

In biblical studies, there is something called the law of first mention. The first mention of a topic in the Bible is given precedence over the understanding and application of that topic when it is mentioned in other parts of the Bible. So, when is "being clothed by God" first mentioned? We will look at three verses in Genesis and discuss their connection to later Scripture.

The man and his wife were both naked, and they felt no shame (Gen. 2:25).

Then the eyes of both were opened, and they realized they were naked... (Gen. 3:7).

The Lord God made garments of skin for Adam and his wife and clothed them (Gen. 3:21).

We may read Genesis 2:25 and think Adam and Eve were not clothed at all, for they were naked and they felt no shame. But with Genesis 3:7, we see there is a connection between their eyes opening and their realization that they were naked. What transpired when their eyes were opened? We will look at that question below. In Genesis 3:21, we read that God is in the business of clothing His people. Was this a new activity for God? Or, in this Scripture, was it just a different material that He used to clothe them?

CLOTHED IN GLORY

Although we know that Adam was made in the image of God, the meaning of this is widely debated—from being free thinking, to being creative, to being emotional, to being kinesthetic; and there are many other meanings attributed to it. But could the image of God also include the qualities seen by the prophet Ezekiel in the image by the Kebar River?

> *Above the expanse over their heads was what looked like a throne of sapphire, and high above on the throne was a figure like that of a Man. I saw that from what appeared to be His waist up He looked like glowing metal, as if full of fire, and that from there down He looked like fire; and brilliant light surrounded Him* (Ezekiel 1:26-27).

This description shows a visual image of God Himself.

Another example of God's visual image is seen in Matthew 17. Here Jesus is transfigured: "*... His face shone like the sun, and His clothes became as white as the light*" (Matt. 17:2). Could Jesus' clothes, at least in the spiritual realm, have actually been made out of the white light and be the same "brilliant light" that Ezekiel had seen?

If Jesus' clothes were white light, then could Adam and Eve, who were made in the image of God, also have had a brilliant light surrounding them in the Garden of Eden? Could they have been naked underneath the brilliant light, which was the glory of God? Was it due to the glory that surrounded them that they could not see their nakedness, because the light was so bright? Could the peace of God have transcended their beings so they flowed in peace, love, and joy, in perfect harmony with each other and with God? I think they were surrounded by that same brilliant light, an attribute of being made in the image of God. But when they sinned, the harmony was lost, and so was the glory of God; the brilliant light that surrounded them disappeared.

Could it have disappeared because they were no longer seeing with their spiritual eyes? These are the eyes of their heart, as Paul calls them in Ephesians 1:18. These are the eyes that seer prophets use to see into the spiritual realm, seers like Ezekiel and John, who saw visions of God and visions of the glory that surrounds the Lord of glory. So Adam and Eve may have seen the glory cloud surrounding themselves before they sinned, since they did not see their own flesh or their nakedness. They only saw the glory of God that surrounded them, for they were made in the image of God (see Gen. 1:26-27). In Matthew, Jesus tells us, *"Blessed are the pure in heart, for they will see God"* (Matt. 5:8). Jesus is telling us that the purity of our heart has to do with our ability to see God, who is Spirit; therefore, this purity of our heart is reflected in our ability to see in the spirit. Adam and Eve lost that ability when they sinned.

So when Genesis 3 says, *"The eyes of both of them were opened, and they realized they were naked,"* it implies that they had begun to see with their natural eyes (Gen. 3:7). These are the eyes we look through to the world around us. Because their spiritual eyes were blinded, they could no longer see the glory around themselves. Instead, they saw their nakedness with their natural eyes. Adam and Eve were indeed blinded, but perhaps it was not only to the light that shone from them; they were also blinded to the light that shone from God. Mark Sandford suggests:

"He was gently calling them, giving them opportunity to repent and thus to be re-clothed in *His* light. But they could not perceive the light of His merciful nature, and hid their nakedness behind the fig leaf of blaming others. If, unlike them, we hearken to God and repent, He will have mercy, and clothe us in light."[1]

This is what I believe happened to them: when their spiritual eyes were opened, they saw the glory clothing themselves, but when they lost the use of those spiritual eyes, they lost the ability to see the glory. Instead, they saw their nakedness with their natural eyes. The pure in heart shall see God (see Matt. 5:8). So, in their purity before the fall, their spiritual eyes were open and they saw God and the glory of God, for *"God is Spirit"* (John 4:24). We will not know if this is true for sure until we talk to them in Heaven or God tells us. However, I think the truth behind this will be substantiated as other Scriptures are examined about the probable reality of being clothed by God.

Another question is—what happened to the glory cloud around them? Did it disappear immediately after they sinned? When their natural eyes opened, did their clothing made of the glory of God simultaneously leave them? Or could it have been that their spiritual eyes were dulled to the spiritual realm of the glory of God, but the glory of God did not leave immediately? They simply could not see the glory of God around their bodies anymore. It may have stayed with them, but they were blind to it. Only later, after they were evicted from the Garden of Eden, was it lost altogether.

When they realized they were naked, they became shameful. So I think that God had originally clothed them in His glory, in His brilliant light, and He had opened their spiritual eyes to see in the spiritual realm. These are traits of being made in the image of God—being clothed in white light and having the spiritual eyes open to see in the heavenly realm.

In Genesis 3, we see that God wanted to clothe them again, but this time it was in inferior garments. They received clothes made from the earthly realm (see Gen. 3:21), not the Designer's clothes, made from the heavenly realm. Choo Thomas, in her book *Heaven is so Real*, tells us that on her visits with Jesus, "He had frequently made changes of His clothes."[2] Perhaps Jesus is behind the fashion designer's creativity, too. This is why I said earlier that I was joking about the devil being behind designer clothes, as that industry can be redeemed by Jesus just as easily as it can be defiled.

When I traveled through North America, Europe, and Africa in my late teens, I occasionally met a person who came across as gentle, kind, and easily likable, and I would see a white light around them. Whenever this happened, I would ask them about their faith, and they would tell me that they were Christians. Now if I could see the Spirit on Christians who were just "believers" and not constantly filled with the Spirit, what would they look like being filled to overflowing with the Holy Spirit? Would they be covered in the armor of light? (See Romans 13:12.)

Concerning the armor of light around believers, I experienced that as a teenager when I saw a light around Christians; I have tangibly felt the presence of God around me; seers told me that they see fire on me or around me; and the Holy Spirit guided me through Scripture regarding the armor of light. All of these incredible experiences have caused me to look at the Scriptures with new eyes, and I now believe there is more truth about Christians being clothed in the Designer's clothes—which is the glory of God—than not. I have listed in Appendix B a number of Scriptures that mention the idea of being clothed by God, and in the remaining chapters of this book, I will continue to mention and discuss other Scriptures in more detail that relate to being clothed by the Spirit. I will now briefly explore Scriptural references on the topic of the glory of God, to see what is revealed to us about being clothed in the Designer's clothes.

~

Discussion Questions

1. In this Chapter, I propose that Adam and Eve were made in the image of God, which included having the light of God around them, like Jesus did. Do you agree with this?

2. Do you think that Jesus, Peter, and Paul were all clothed in the glory of God while on earth?

3. Discuss how you have felt the Holy Spirit filling you. Do you have the same or different manifestations as Paul when he describes how he struggles with the Holy Spirit's energy that works so powerfully within him?

    * Have you felt or experienced either of these sensations Paul describes?

ENDNOTES

1. Mark Sandford, "Suggestions" e-mail, December 30, 2009.

2. Choo Thomas, *Heaven is so Real* (Lake Mary, FL: Charisma House, 2006), 163.

CHAPTER 6

THE GLORY OF GOD

*In the year that King Uzziah died, I saw the Lord seated on a throne,
high and exalted, and the train of His robe filled the temple. Above
Him were seraphs, each with six wings: With two wings they covered
their faces, with two they covered their feet, and with two they were
flying. And they were calling to one another: "Holy, holy, holy is the
Lord Almighty; the whole earth is full of His glory." At the sound of
their voices the doorposts and thresholds shook and the temple was
filled with smoke* (Isaiah 6:1-4).

*So I got up and went out to the plain. And the glory of the Lord was
standing there, like the glory I had seen by the Kebar River, and I fell
face down* (Ezekiel 3:23).

*Then the glory of the Lord rose from above the cherubim and moved to
the threshold of the temple. The cloud filled the temple, and the court
was full of the radiance of the glory of the Lord* (Ezekiel 10:4).

The glory of the Lord went up from within the city and stopped above the mountain east of it (Ezekiel 11:23).

In this chapter I will discuss the glory of God, also known as the glory of the Lord. This can be an expansive topic, so I will only make a few points in this book. There are two Hebrew words for "glory." One is *kawbode,* and it means the weightiness of God's presence, as seen in Second Chronicles 5:14, where we read that the priests could not stand under the weight of God's glory. Figuratively, it is God's splendor, His copiousness, and His honor.[1] The other Hebrew word for glory, found in Habakkuk 3:3, is *hode,* which means grandeur—an imposing form which has an appearance of beauty, excellence, honor, and majesty.[2] Both Hebrew words describe the attributes of God and give us the sense of the majestic personhood of the exalted Lord Jesus Christ.

"IT" OR "HE"

The first point about the glory of God that I want to make is found in Isaiah 6:1-4, where the prophet Isaiah is taken into a heavenly vision and sees God on His throne. Isaiah describes God's garments as a *robe,* and describes that robe's train as filling the temple (see Isa. 6:1, quoted at the start of this chapter). Now, something "fills" something else by occupying it wholly or by putting as much as possible into it, appearing to leave no room for anything else. But was the train of God's robe still in the temple when the smoke appeared? Or was God just showing us another dimension of His glory by showing us the smoke?

I find it very interesting that the robe transitioned into smoke. God is clothed in a robe, and that robe may possibly be reflecting His glory, so it is also seen as smoke. The seraphs declare that God is "Holy, holy, holy" because He is so complex and awesome that He keeps revealing more of who He is, and He can manifest Himself to the rest of creation. The seraphs are compelled to say He is holy, meaning He is set apart and so different from the rest of the created universe. Therefore, the robe of God turning into smoke is just another one of the dimensional shifts that God makes to show the observer more of who He is and how awesome He is.

The other observation I want to point out about the glory of God is from Ezekiel 1, where the prophet sees high above the throne a figure that looks like a man, and that man has a brilliant light surrounding Him. We recognize the Man as the exalted Lord Jesus Christ (see Ezek. 1:26).

Then the prophet says, *"This was the appearance of the likeness of the glory of the Lord"* (Ezek. 1:28). Therefore, Ezekiel identifies the appearance of the glory of the Lord with the figure of a Man, the Lord Jesus Christ. This is significant, as I personally have at times minimized my experience of being in the anointing or in the presence of God. I realize that I have been a bit dull to the omnipresent powers of the Lord; and at times I do not give the Lord adequate recognition and worship when the presence of God is around me, for I have been dulled to it, and I have been asleep to the presence of God.

Interestingly, in Ezekiel 3 the prophet describes, *"And the glory of Lord was standing there…"* and this word usage gives the glory the attribute of a person who stands (Ezek. 3:23). This is again how we associate the figure of the Man with the Lord Jesus Christ, who is the Lord of glory (see 1 Cor. 2:8).

A few chapters later, Ezekiel 9:3 refers to the glory of God having moved from where "it" had been sitting—as translated in the NIV and the NET Bible—but the King James Version refers to the glory of God with the pronoun "He." This verse says the glory was sitting, which is an attribute of the Man—the Son of Man, Jesus Christ—but what I find strange is that the NIV and the NET Bible use "it." This translation makes it look like Ezekiel depersonalizes this reference to the glory of God by saying an "it" had been sitting there. I am struck that when the glory of the Lord is mentioned in other verses of Ezekiel, these translations do not seem to properly represent how we should honor the glory of the Lord. Other verses just talk about the glory of the Lord doing something, instead of addressing Him more personally.

WHO HE IS

The glory of the Lord is the Lord Jesus Christ, the firstborn Son of God. Wherever He goes, the glory of the Lord goes, for the glory is Jesus Christ and it is the radiance of Him being God. I do not want to be asleep and unaware that Jesus Christ Himself is living in me and is around me by His Spirit. Like Paul teaches, a man and wife are united and become one flesh; this is *"a profound mystery,"* which is Christ in us, the *"hope of glory"* (see Eph. 5:32; Col. 1:27).

I was really asleep before to the reality that Christ, the hope of glory, was actually living in me. Consequently, I need to be diligent and fight off this sleep and know He is with me. In my early revelation, I shared what Jesus said: *"... And surely I am with you always, to the very end of the age"* (Matt. 28:20). This is a greater and more intimate revelation for me today than it was a few years ago. But I still constantly battle the tendency to reduce the anointing of God's presence or shrink the glory of the Lord to being just an "it."

Martin Buber, in his book *I and Thou*, wrote about the tendency in Christian communities to have "I-it" relationships, instead of "I-Thou" or "I-You" relationships. Many of us have made our relationship with the Lord Jesus Christ and others "I-it" relationships.[3]

But Jesus prayed:

Now this is eternal life: that they may know You, the only true God, and Jesus Christ, whom You have sent (John 17:3).

To know and be known is ultimately important in all relationships. "Knowing" is the Greek word *ginosko,* and it means, "to know cognitively, to be aware, to know, to feel, to perceive, to be resolved, to be sure, and to understand."[4] But it also derives a meaning from Matthew 1:25, which says Joseph did not "know" Mary until after Jesus was born. The Greek word is still *ginosko,* and it holds the same meaning in the Hebrew language as in Genesis, where, *"Adam knew Eve"* (Gen. 4:1 KJV). The implication for both of these verses is the intimate knowing through a sexual union. This is a metaphor, as our Lord does not want a sexual union with us—even though we are the Bride of Christ—but Jesus wants a spiritual union with us by entering us with His Spirit. He derives joy from His chosen children who allow Him to fill their bodies, souls, and spirits with His Spirit, as this is the profound mystery that Paul alluded to (see Eph. 5:32). This profound mystery is that the Spirit gives birth to our spirit, so we become children of God! And that is what we are! (See John 3:6; 1:13; 1 John 3:1.)

KNOWING HIM

I need to wake up to the fact that Jesus Christ lives in me, and I live in Him. As I probed earlier in this book I wondered, "How do I live in Jesus?" Well, as I received the revelation that the Holy Spirit was all over me and clothing me, He answered my questions as to how I was in Jesus, for I was clothed in the Designer's clothes—in Christ's glory, for God is light (see 1 John 1:5). So now I can no longer take His presence and the glory of God as an "it" or just a "power." Instead, I have the divine partnership with the Lord Jesus Christ, who is working through me to accomplish all that He planned for me to accomplish. Jesus is in me and Jesus surrounds me. He has to be in me and surround me, because He said that *"... apart from Me you can do nothing"* (John 15:5). Therefore, I now have the revelation that His presence is literally within me and surrounds me.

I do not want to have an impersonal relationship with God. I want to know Him, live in Him, and have Him live in me. I want to wake up to the reality that I live in Jesus, and He lives in me. So I had to repent for the dullness of my heart.

If you can relate to being a bit dull to recognizing the glory of God as the presence of Jesus Christ Himself, then you may need to pray this prayer of repentance:

> *Heavenly Father, I confess that, at times, I have been asleep and inattentive to Your Holy presence, to Your Holy Spirit, to the Lord Jesus Christ. I have had an "I-it" relationship with You and with Your presence, so please forgive me for dishonoring You and Your presence.* [Pause for 10 seconds and reflect on what you just prayed.]
>
> *I receive Your forgiveness now. Thank You, Lord Jesus, for Your blood that washes away my sin.* [Pause and reflect.]
>
> *Father, please give me the grace to wake up and help me start a new quest of thirst and hunger for You. I do want to know You and serve You and love You. I want Your divine life in me, and I want to be in You. I want to be intimate with You, my God. Jesus, You said that if I remain in You, and You remain in me, there will be much fruit* (see John 15:5). *I want You, Jesus, to help me to remain in You, and I invite You to remain in me. I want to know You, to be filled by Your Spirit, to be fruitful, and to glorify Your name. Amen.*

~

Discussion Questions

1. Isaiah 6:3 says, *"... The whole earth is full of His glory."* Discuss your level of awareness of this reality.

    ❧ How do you see the whole earth full of His glory?

    ❧ We can imagine cell phone, television, and radio signals; they are real, yet they move through the atmosphere unseen. How does this help you understand the spiritual realm, and how might the glory of God also be in our atmosphere but remain unseen?

2. Discuss whether you, too, tend to grow more and more impersonal in your relationship to God and your view of the anointing or His presence or His glory.

    ❧ Are you intimate with God, or do you struggle getting close and connected to God?

    ❧ Whom do you pray to?

    ❧ Do you struggle with praying to any of the three persons of the Trinity?

    ❧ Do you have "I-it" relationships? How can they be changed to "I-Thou" relationships?

    ❧ Do you think you can have an "I-it" relationship with people and an "I-Thou" relationship with God?

3. Discuss how you want to know God more.

ENDNOTES

1. Strong, *The Exhaustive Concordance* (H1935).

2. Strong, *The Exhaustive Concordance* (H3519).

3. Martin Buber, *I and Thou*. Trans. by Walter Kaufmann. (New York, NY: Charles Scribner's Sons, 1970), 62-72; 177-182.

4. Strong, *The Exhaustive Concordance* (G1097).

CHAPTER 7

THE FULL ARMOR OF GOD

Finally, be strong in the Lord and in His mighty power. Put on the full armor of God so that you can take your stand against the devil's schemes. For our struggle is not against flesh and blood, but against the rulers, against the authorities, against the powers of this dark world and against the spiritual forces of evil in the heavenly realms. Therefore put on the full armor of God, so that when the day of evil comes, you may be able to stand your ground, and after you have done everything, to stand. Stand firm then, with the belt of truth buckled around your waist, with the breastplate of righteousness in place, and with your feet fitted with the readiness that comes from the gospel of peace. In addition to all this, take up the shield of faith, with which you can extinguish the flaming arrows of the evil one. Take the helmet of salvation and the sword of the Spirit, which is the word of God. And pray in the Spirit on all occasions with all kinds of prayers and requests. With this in mind, be alert and always keep on praying for all the saints (Ephesians 6:10-18).

Paul was under house arrest in Rome when he wrote in his letter to the Ephesians, *"Put on the full armor of God so that you can take your stand against the devil's schemes"* (Eph. 6:11). Outside his doorway was stationed a Roman guard wearing armor, likely inspiring Paul's writings in Ephesians 6. However, *"Put on the full armor of God"* should also be read in the context of the previous chapter in Ephesians, in which Paul wrote, *"... be filled with the Spirit"* (Eph. 5:18). Do you remember that Paul was the apostle who had handkerchiefs and napkins touch his body, and from them people received healing and their demons left them? He did that in Ephesus (see Acts 19:12). He also wrote in Colossians: *"To this end I labor, struggling with all His energy, which so powerfully works in me"* (Col. 1:29). Paul experienced being full of the Holy Spirit's power as the Holy Spirit worked in him and through him.

I also can attest that the Holy Spirit filled my legs and my arms, rested heavily on my torso, and covered my head and face, specifically on my forehead and nose. I wondered, "Is this a helmet in the spiritual realm?" Barbara Parker's testimony in Appendix C says she discerned I had something like "a Roman helmet from biblical times" on me. My experience has been that the armor of God has literally clothed me. The only thing I did not feel was the Holy Spirit on my back. This is how it was with the Roman soldier's armor—his back was not covered with armor, but he was girded on the front of his legs, arms, torso, and head.

I believe Paul felt the Holy Spirit around himself the way I have, because he said, *"In Him we live and move and have our being... "* (Acts 17:28). This appears to be Paul describing living in a cloud of Glory. Paul may also have seen the Holy Spirit around himself. So when he looked at the Roman soldier, he realized that visual image gave him a language, a metaphor for what it felt like for him to be filled to overflowing with the Spirit of God. Paul may have felt like he was cloaked in the full armor of God. What I call the Designer's clothes includes aspects of the full armor of God, which is a spiritual coat of God's armor and protection. The definition of the Designer's clothes given later in Chapter Nine covers the aspect of the full armor of God, along with additional functions of the Designer's clothes. But these functions are not found in the description of the full armor of God.

Personally, I have felt uncomfortable when people suggest we should "mime" putting on the garments of God's armor. Now that I am filled with the Holy Spirit, I can see why I felt uncomfortable. It was because God intended to clothe us when we are filled to overflowing with the Holy Spirit. Miming putting on the armor of God can be a prophetic act when done in faith, and can have the beneficial effect of building trust in God's protection. But I believe the real armor of God was intended to be the result of being filled by the Spirit to overflowing. Paul says the armor is to help you *"take your stand against the devil's schemes"* (Eph. 6:11). I have a testimony about how God's armor did that for me.

SHIELD OF PROTECTION

After I conducted a training session with the healing rooms, one of the prophetic intercessors suggested that I should receive prayer. She said, "Since Neil is the leader of this ministry, he is prone to spiritual attacks." So they prayed for me, and I went home. When I got home, I went down to the basement to soak in a place that was next to the furnace. When I lay down on the mat, I smelled a foul smell. I had a series of thoughts: "Is it the furnace making the smell?" No. "Did I mess myself?" No, that wasn't it. "Hmm, didn't someone say that demons often emit bad odors?"

With that realization, I immediately said, "I command you, foul spirit, to leave right now, in Jesus' name." And the odor began to disappear. The next night I went down to soak and I smelled the same odor, so immediately I said, "I command you right now, you foul spirit, to leave, in Jesus' name." And the odor disappeared.

I had realized that the prophetic intercessor had heard correctly, and I was thankful for their prayers. Then, about three months later, I sat facing the computer in my office and smelled the odor again, and I said, "Get out of here, you foul spirit, in Jesus' name, go!" And it left. The evil spirit never got to me or hurt me. God was showing me how He protected me from the devil, because I did everything to take my stand against the devil's schemes—I had asked the Spirit to fill me with His presence and to overshadow me, I woke up to the discernment that the evil spirit was near me, and then I commanded it to go. Standing is not being passive, but it is building a bulwark with steps of faith.

I believe I had the armor of God on, for not only had I soaked regularly, but I had also declared Psalm 91 over my life every day, saying, *"I will say of the Lord, 'He is my refuge and my fortress, my God, in whom I trust'"* (Ps. 91:2). So I found myself in the school of the Holy Spirit again, and He was teaching me about the armor of God and how God was protecting me. He had opened my nose up to the spiritual realm, so I could smell the demon around me. But the demon could not attack me, because God was my *"shield and rampart"* (see Ps. 91:4). He also wanted to teach me about my authority over demons because of my being in Christ. The devil's scheme was to torment me, but God turned it around and used it to train me to come against the devil and his schemes, and to show me that He surrounded me with His glory.

Saul experienced the opposite of what I did. Saul was protected by the Spirit of the Lord, as were all the kings of Israel. So Saul was protected from evil spirits when the Spirit was upon him. But we read that *"the Spirit of the Lord had departed from Saul, and an evil spirit from the Lord tormented him"* (1 Sam. 16:14). Because the Holy Spirit had left Saul, the evil spirit had access to him. Thankfully, we live in the new covenant today. In the old covenant, only prophets and kings had the Holy Spirit's protection, but now all believers can have access to God's protection with the overshadowing of the Holy Spirit that creates an armor of light around us. But this is only possible if we have asked for the Holy Spirit to fill us and to overshadow us.

THE ARMOR OF LIGHT

Paul was not like Saul, for he was a man of the Spirit. I have no doubt that the Spirit was all around him. Acts describes Paul as performing extraordinary miracles while he was in Ephesus (see Acts 19:11). It must have been an amazing testimony time for Paul. His renown must have spread throughout the region. Undoubtedly, people would have flocked to him and asked him, "How did the handkerchief that you had on your body heal the sick and free people from their demons?"

What did Paul say to these inquiring Ephesians? Maybe Paul told them, "I am covered with God's glory," or, "I am covered with God's protection." Maybe he even said that he was covered by "the armor of light." Regardless of what he told them, Paul was clearly a man full of the Holy Spirit.

Paul wrote in his letter to the Romans, which predates the letter to the Ephesians, *"Put on the armor of light"* and *"Clothe yourselves with the Lord Jesus Christ"* (Rom. 13:12,14). So maybe he told the Ephesians, "I am clothed in the armor of light, which is the Lord Jesus Christ Himself!"

Whatever he said, it would point to Christ and declare that He was with him. For Paul had told the Romans to be clothed in Christ. Paul knew from his Damascus road experience that God is light (see Acts 9:3-4). Paul also knew that God's light covers believers like armor, so he wrote, *"Put on the armor of light"* (Rom. 13:12). Paul had already thought of believers putting on the armor of God and being clothed in Jesus Christ before he wrote the letter to the Ephesians, in which he told them to *"live as children of light"* (Eph. 5:8). So I believe the phrase *"the full armor of God"* was another way for Paul to say what he said to the Romans, which is to put on Jesus Christ and the armor of light.

It appears obvious that Paul would have conceptualized the full armor of God being made of light. So when he wrote about the full armor of God in Ephesians, he had most likely visualized it with his spiritual eyes as an "armor of light," for he prayed for the Ephesians *"that the eyes of your heart may be enlightened"* (Eph. 1:18). I believe it is reasonable to conclude that Paul had both felt and seen the armor of light around believers, so when he was living in Ephesus, he encouraged believers to be clothed in God's light and God's armor.

When Paul saw a Roman soldier at his door in Rome, it may have been the stimulus for him to begin to write to the church in Ephesus. It may have triggered his memory of having told them he had been clothed in the *"armor of light"* (Rom. 13:12). Paul may have remembered that he wanted to remind them that they too should be clothed in the armor of light and in Jesus Christ. The Ephesians heard Paul's own testimony that he had been clothed in Jesus Christ, which explained why his handkerchiefs were taken to people, and they were healed and their demons were driven out.

Paul wanted to add to that idea of being clothed in light, so he added the word "full" to the previous ideas of the armor of light or the armor of God. He said, *"put on the full armor of God,"* which includes the power for protection against the devil's schemes and also includes the inner work that the Spirit does within believers. The Spirit fills believers with the fruit of the Spirit, as well as other character qualities (see Gal. 5:22). The Spirit builds in them the traits of truth, righteousness, and peace that Paul writes about in Ephesians 6. It is critical for us to see that the full armor of God from Ephesians 6 is linked to the previous chapter that says *"be filled with the Spirit"* (Eph. 5:18). For if there is no filling of the Spirit, then there is no armor of God. Therefore, Paul indicates that the idea of being "full" addresses the personality issues of believers, as it represents both the inner character transformation of the believer and the filling and overshadowing of the Spirit who protects the believer from the devil's schemes.

So if the believer puts on *"the full armor of God,"* Paul is telling us we should cloak our being with God's glory, God's light, and God's Holy Spirit. The believer is just like Paul, Peter, and Jesus, who were all clothed in the glory of God by the Holy Spirit, for they all wore the Designer's clothes.

Psalm 91 declares that God will save us from the deadly pestilence, the fowler's snare, terror, arrows, and plagues, so that no harm will befall us. God will protect us, deliver us, and allow us to walk over the lion, the cobra, and the serpent. Clearly, it depicts God as the One who surrounds us with His wings, protects us, and shields us from the devil and his schemes.

James writes, *"Submit yourselves, then, to God. Resist the devil, and he will flee from you. Come near to God and He will come near to you…"* (James 4:7-8). We put on the full armor of God by being overshadowed by the Holy Spirit—which is the same thing as coming near to God— and resisting the devil. Submitting and coming near to God are two of the three things that James teaches for spiritual warfare. So submitting and coming near to God are similar to asking the Holy Spirit to fill you and clothe you each and every day. Being filled with God's Spirit is coming as near to God as you possibly can. And James also writes that we are to resist the devil and he will flee, and that is like saying, "Get out of here, you foul spirit, in Jesus' name." The devil will flee from you when you exercise your authority and tell him to go.

Putting on the full armor of God is a metaphor Paul used to empha-size an important theme he brought out in the letter to the Ephesians. As I wrote earlier in Chapter Two, in every chapter of Ephesians, Paul men-tions or implies that believers should be filled with the Holy Spirit. And he means they need to be continually filled to overflowing, until each be-liever has a shadow of the Holy Spirit around him, creating the full armor of God. In this way, they can take their own handkerchiefs and aprons to others who will receive healing; in addition, believers will receive God's protection from demonic attacks and receive the transformation of their characters by putting on the Designer's clothes.

Discussion Questions

1. In reading Ephesians 6:11 before, what did you think the full armor of God was?

   - Did you think it was something you needed to understand mentally?

   - Did you think it was something you needed to put on yourself like a suit of clothes in the morning?

   - Did you ever think of yourself as having to *put on the armor of light,*" as Paul says in Romans 13:12?

   - Did you think it told you to do something like *"clothe yourselves with the Lord Jesus Christ"* (Rom. 13:14)?

2. Do you agree that Paul was trying to encourage the Ephesians to be filled with the Holy Spirit and cloaked in the armor of light, which he called the full armor of God (see Eph. 6:11)?

   - If not, what else was he trying to teach them?

3. How have you found success in standing against demonic attacks?

   - Have you ever smelled a foul smell and not known what it was?

   - Discuss possible discernment experiences you may have had regarding smells.

   - Discuss if you have ever had discernment for demons in any other ways beside smell.

CHAPTER 8

ASKING TO BE CLOTHED

And why do you worry about clothes? See how the lilies of the field grow. They do not labor or spin. Yet I tell you that not even Solomon in all his splendor was dressed like one of these. If that is how God clothes the grass of the field, which is here today and tomorrow is thrown into the fire, will He not much more clothe you, O you of little faith? So do not worry, saying "What shall we eat?" or "What shall we drink?" or "What shall we wear?" For the pagans run after all these things, and your heavenly Father knows that you need them. But seek first His Kingdom and His righteousness, and all these things will be given to you as well. Therefore do not worry about tomorrow, for tomorrow will worry about itself. Each day has enough trouble of its own (Matthew 6:28-34).

I had been made aware of the Holy Spirit's presence around me, so I started to look for other Scriptures to help me understand my experiences. I found Matthew 6, which says:

And why do you worry about clothes? ...Will He not much more clothe you, O you of little faith? (Matthew 6:28,30)

Then, a couple of verses later, Jesus says,

"But seek first His Kingdom and His righteousness, and all these things will be given to you as well" (Matthew 6:33).

Did you notice the question that Jesus asked above: *"Will He not much more clothe you?"* Jesus was challenging the disciples' faith to believe that the Father wanted to clothe them. What does the Father want to clothe you with? Well, the key to receiving the clothing is what Jesus said—to *"seek first His Kingdom"* and seek it with faith. So what is the Kingdom of God comprised of?

THE KINGDOM OF GOD

Jesus tells us in Luke, *"If I drive out demons by the finger of God, then the Kingdom of God has come to you,"* and He also said that *"the Kingdom of God is within you"* (Luke 11:20; 17:21). The experience I had with the Holy Spirit flowing out of my fingers, causing demons to leave people, occurred only because I soaked in the presence of the Holy Spirit day after day until the Kingdom of God was formed within me. (See Jodi's testimony in Appendix C.) So when we seek the Kingdom of God, we are seeking the Holy Spirit to fill us. When the Holy Spirit fills us, then the Kingdom of God is within us, and then God can pour out through us.

As we continually seek the Kingdom, the Father will also begin to slowly clothe us with the Holy Spirit. The phrase, *"O you of little faith,"* actually refers to God promising us that He will clothe us. Jesus implies that He is asking us, "Do you really believe that the Father wants to clothe you, too? Do you believe that if you earnestly seek the Kingdom of God which is the Holy Spirit, the Father will clothe you? Do you have little or big faith for this?"

Jesus touched this point again with the disciples when He said, *"I am going to send you what My Father promised; but stay in the city until you have been clothed with power from on high"* (Luke 24:49). Jesus reminded them of the Father's promise to clothe them! When this revelation came into my spirit and I had understanding, I leapt up in faith and began to declare:

> *Father in Heaven, Your Word says if I seek the Kingdom of God then You will clothe me. So I ask in Jesus' name that You will clothe me in Your presence. Overshadow me, Father, just like You overshadowed Peter. Make me a habitation of Your glory, let me be a light, a brilliant light that shines for Your sake, Father, and also that I may glorify Jesus and make Him famous.*

The result from praying and declaring that Scripture back to the Father was that I began to feel an increase of the presence of God around me. More and more I had an increase of the intensity of heat coming out of my hands. The fire of God increased in my life, and so did the Kingdom. Again, I felt as if this was what I was made for. I had been waiting all my life to manifest the Kingdom of God, and now, finally, the obstacles were being overcome. I was beginning to walk in my birthright as the man of God He had made me to be.

FOUND IN HIM

In addition to seeking the Kingdom of God, Jesus also said to seek His righteousness. So how do we seek His righteous? I think that believers who seek His righteousness first have to make an identity shift. That shift is due to us being found in Christ, as Paul says:

*I consider everything a loss compared to the surpassing greatness of knowing Christ Jesus my Lord, for whose sake I have lost all things. I consider them rubbish, that I may gain Christ and **be found in Him**, not having a righteousness of my own that comes from the law, but that which is through faith in Christ—**the righteousness that comes from God and is by faith*** (Philippians 3:8-9).

Our righteousness comes from being found in Christ and by having faith. So when we are in Christ, by faith He makes us righteous. First John says, *"No one who lives in Him keeps on sinning"* (1 John 3:6). If we live in Jesus Christ we become righteous, for it is the Holy Spirit that makes the Gentiles an offering acceptable to God, because we are sanctified by the Holy Spirit. Sanctified means to be made holy (see Rom. 15:16). We have a wonderful Savior who will make us holy because He is holy. So pursuing His righteousness is not a religious work, but it is a response to the wooing of the Spirit of God who changes us from the inside out. So pursuing His Kingdom, which is the Holy Spirit, is the same thing as pursuing His righteousness, since His righteousness comes out of pursuing His Kingdom.

The Holy Spirit will make us holy and righteous if we yield to Him; then we will be clothed in Jesus Christ and He will be our righteousness, for He is the Designer's clothes we put on. This is the process the Lord wants all believers to take to have us filled by the Holy Spirit so we are transformed by the power of God, and we learn to be clothed in Jesus Christ by putting on the Designer's clothes.

~

Discussion Questions

1. Matthew 6:28-30 may imply that God wants us to ask Him to clothe us in His glory.

    ❧ Discuss how you used to think about this Scripture.

    ❧ Discuss how thinking about the Scripture in the way presented in this book requires a different response from you.

2. Decreeing Scripture is one of the keys in walking in the Kingdom and in your birthright.

    ❧ Discuss what Scriptures you have decreed before.

    ❧ Discuss what Scriptures you would like to decree.

3. What is the difference between prayer and decrees?

CHAPTER 9

DEFINING THE DESIGNER'S CLOTHES

... He was transfigured before them. His clothes became dazzling white, whiter than anyone in the world could bleach them (Mark 9:2-3).

I have used the name "the Designer's clothes" for the key term in this book and its main theme, for a couple of reasons. First, the creation-based, scientific model called Intelligent Design argues that the makeup of the creation is beyond chance. Intelligent Design concludes that the creation points to a Creator. But its supporters do not use the term Creator; they use the less controversial term "Designer." And since this book is talking about the spiritual clothes that God wants to put on us, the term Designer fits very well into this theme. It also plays off the contemporary terminology for fashion designers, who make clothes. Fashion designer is written with a small "d," but the term Designer with a big "D" refers to none other than the Lord Jesus Christ. Scripture tells us that, *"Through Him all things were made; without Him nothing was made that has been made"* (John 1:3).

Since Jesus Christ is the ultimate Designer and the Creator of the whole creation, the "D" of Designer is capitalized as it denotes the Lord Jesus Christ, the Creator God. It is often the practice to capitalize the names or pronouns that address God, so the Designer is capitalized. The possessive form—Designer's—is used to imply that the clothes actually belong to Jesus Christ, but since believers are joint heirs with Christ, we also may have access to the same wardrobe that Jesus wears (see Rom. 8:17).

The plurality of the term "the Designer's clothes" is because although there is only one Designer—Jesus Christ—every single believer can wear their own set of Designer's clothes; therefore, there are millions of sets of Designer's clothes. There is a set for each and every Spirit-filled believer to wear. The clothes are plural due to the number of sets that can be worn. Now, for the definition of the Designer's clothes, we must look at both the earthly and heavenly garments that Jesus Christ wore, as found in Scripture.

THE SON OF MAN

When I was looking at the Scriptures surrounding Jesus' life, I found it interesting that there are few references to His clothing, yet the Son of Man appeared to have many people attracted to His clothing.

Mark says that people begged Jesus to let them *"touch even the edge of His cloak,"* and all who touched Him got healed (Mark 6:56). I find it fascinating that they *begged* Him to touch His clothes. Why did they not beg to touch Him? Why did they not beg Him to touch *them?* Did touching His clothes allow them to touch His power? Apparently it did, because they were healed. The woman with the blood issue is one person who touched Jesus' clothes. She is said to have come *"up behind Him... and touched His cloak,"* as she had already thought, *"If I just touch His clothes, I will be healed"* (Mark 5:27-28). Again, touching His clothes ran through her mind. Why? What was the attraction to Jesus' clothes?

Interestingly, Jesus had discernment when the woman with the blood issue came up behind Him and touched His clothes (see Mark 5:30). But how could He feel her touching His clothes? In my personal experience of imparting the Holy Spirit to people by pointing my fingers at their fingers from a distance, I have found that, when they begin to engage in a greater level of faith, I feel them pulling the anointing out of me with their faith, and it flows with increased force and intensity. Since the woman came up and touched His clothes *in faith*, she may have done the same thing and pulled the power out of Jesus with her faith; consequently, Jesus felt the rush of power being pulled out of His body. Jesus confirms this idea with His statement, *"Daughter, your faith has healed you"* (Mark 5:34). Her faith pulled the healing power out of Jesus and brought her the healing she was looking for. Therefore, I believe that, even though He did not feel His body being touched, Jesus discerned by feeling the power leaving Him. I think He had the same experience with other people who would just touch His clothes or touch Him, or He would touch them—He would feel the power pulled out through His body because they exercised their faith.

Another group of people wanted Jesus' clothes after His death. In the Gospel of John, we read that the Roman soldiers noted Jesus' *"undergarment... was seamless, woven in one piece from top to bottom"* (John 19:23). So they elected not to tear it, but drew lots to see who got it. I wonder about this, since clothes that touched Paul's body were carried off to heal people and drive demons away, and certainly something that Jesus wore would do the same thing. Surely Jesus' clothes were permeated with the anointing of the Holy Spirit, and they would heal the sick and cast out demons and possibly even release peace and joy. Maybe the soldiers felt so good when they were near Jesus' clothes that their muscles began to relax, and their pain left their bodies along with their demons. That is why they bartered for the garments of Jesus, because they felt something really good happening to them when they were near Jesus' clothes. Each of them wanted the undergarment for himself. Maybe they were also somehow attracted to the atmosphere it created? People were attracted to Jesus' clothes whether he had them on or not.

The isolated strips of Jesus' clothing in the empty tomb speak of a different message. The strips of linen and the burial cloth lay folded up, but these clothes only speak of the absence of Jesus' body—He is risen! (See John 20:7.) The burial clothes may have had a slight residual anointing on the cloth, but only an infinitesimal amount compared to the overshadowing of the Holy Spirit that Jesus had when He walked on the earth, which was on the seamless undergarment Jesus had worn daily. But the burial clothes had been around Jesus' body for only a few days, and it was after He had died—His spirit had been taken from the body. So very little if any of the anointing would have permeated those clothes and that was only possible if some of the anointing had remained in Jesus' bones. Anointing could have come from Jesus' bones, for Elisha's bones could raise the dead (see 2 Kings 13:21). But Jesus' body had risen—no bones about it. So only a residual amount of anointing was probably on the folded burial cloth. That is why it is the only time His clothing is mentioned in Scripture when people did not clamor to touch it. In John 20 we read that both John and Peter looked at the strips of linen, but they were not compelled to touch Jesus' burial clothes, because Jesus had risen. The Spirit had left Him. His spiritual clothing was taken—the Designer's clothes had been taken from Jesus, the last Adam, just like the Designer's clothes had been taken from the first Adam (see 1 Cor. 15:45; Gen. 3:7).

Jesus, when He was ministering on earth, displayed another set of clothes that was revealed when "*... He was transfigured before them. His clothes became dazzling white, whiter than anyone in the world could bleach* *them"* (Mark 9:2-3). It is also noted that *"... His face shone like the sun, and His clothes became as white as the light"* (Matt. 17:2). Perhaps the transfiguration was only an opening of the spiritual eyes of the disciples to see the reality that was there all the time? Perhaps Jesus' clothes were actually white light? The disciples' spiritual eyes were opened, and they saw the spiritual reality that had always been there but had been hidden from their natural eyes.

Perhaps Jesus' clothes of white light infused the undergarment and made it very attractive to the soldiers. The clothes of white light were around Jesus, and that was why people begged to touch His clothes—because they were touching part of the Kingdom of God when they touched the white light that surrounded Jesus. We see this same white light also surrounds the Lord Jesus Christ when He is in the heavenly realm.

THE EXALTED LORD

... High above on the throne was a figure like that of a Man. I saw that from what appeared to be His waist up He looked like glowing metal, as if full of fire, and that from there down He looked like fire; and brilliant light surrounded Him (Ezekiel 1:26-27).

In the next verse, Ezekiel describes this as *"the appearance of the likeness of the glory of the Lord"* (Ezek. 1:28). The glory of the Lord is like the Man that John writes about in Revelation, for he saw:

... someone "like a son of man"... His eyes were like blazing fire. His feet were like bronze glowing in a furnace... and out of His mouth came a sharp double-edged sword. His face was like the sun shining in all its brilliance (Revelation 1:13-16).

John's book is also known as the Revelation of Jesus Christ. The glory of the Lord is the Lord Jesus Christ. Like Jesus in the transfiguration, a brilliant white light surrounds Him, and fire is in His eyes and is all around Him.

From these previous examples of Scripture, we read that Jesus' garments show up as glory or brilliant light. This helps me to now define the visual appearance of the Designer's clothes.

THE DESIGNER'S CLOTHES DEFINED VISUALLY

From the Scriptures on the previous pages we see Jesus' clothing was in both the natural and the supernatural. We also see that it was attractive to people, and that it was like a brilliant white light that surrounded Him. This surrounding light is the manifestation of the glory of the Lord that Ezekiel saw. The glory was also seen as a cloud that filled the temple and *"... the court was full of the radiance of the glory of the Lord"* (Ezek. 10:4).

This brilliant white light that surrounds like a cloud is the glory of God, and it is the visual appearance of the Designer's clothes if we had eyes to see it. I believe Peter's shadow looked like this brilliant white light that surrounded Peter like a cloud or a shadow (see Acts 5:15). The Designer's clothes, I believe, were also worn by Adam and Eve in the Garden of Eden before the Fall. Being made in the image of God includes having the brilliant light of God around us. The Designer's clothes look like a brilliant white light that reflects the radiance of the glory of the Lord. But how do the Designer's clothes function?

THE DESIGNER'S CLOTHES DEFINED FUNCTIONALLY

Jesus read His mandate from Isaiah 61:

The Spirit of the Lord is on Me, because He has anointed Me to preach good news to the poor. He has sent Me to proclaim freedom for the prisoners and recovery of sight for the blind, to release the oppressed, to proclaim the year of the Lord's favor (Luke 4:18-19).

When Jesus read this mandate, it was after He had returned in the power of the Holy Spirit from the desert. Good news to the poor, proclamations of freedom, the blind seeing, and the release of the oppressed are all the results of Jesus' power and authority due to being clothed in power from the Holy Spirit. So those who wear the Designer's clothes are called to function by doing the same things that Jesus was assigned to do in His mandate from Luke. And those who wear the Designer's clothes also need to be clothed with power from on high in order to do what Jesus has mandated us to do.

The purpose of the Designer's clothes includes those functions found in the full armor of God. Paul implies that the armor protects the believer from the devil's schemes, and enables the believer to extinguish fiery darts of the enemy (see Eph. 6:16). Also, the filling of the Spirit brings character development to the believer, who is filled with truth, righteousness, peace, and faith. The Designer's clothes include both the functions of protection and character maturity from the full armor of God. However, there is more to the Designer's clothes than what is described with the full armor of God.

POWER AND AUTHORITY

"... *The power of the Lord was present for Him to heal the sick*" (Luke 5:17). This power will surround those wearing the Designer's clothes. Paul and Peter wore the Designer's clothes, and Paul said:

...Christ has accomplished through me in leading the Gentiles to obey God by what I have said and done—by the power of signs and miracles through the power of the Spirit... (Romans 15:18-19).

Those who wear the Designer's clothes will also see signs and miracles being performed around them as they minister. This power includes the power to raise the dead too (see Matt. 10:8; John 11:43-44).

Those wearing the Designer's clothes will also carry the authority of Christ: *"All authority in Heaven and on earth has been given to Me. Therefore go and make disciples of all nations... "* (Matt. 28:18-19). When we remain in Jesus and He remains in us, it is then that authority is given to us and we can go and produce lots of fruit (see John 15:5). The authority for deliverance is also given as Jesus said:

> *I have given you authority to trample on snakes and scorpions and to overcome all the power of the enemy; nothing will harm you* (Luke 10:19).

And this authority also includes *"the keys to the Kingdom of Heaven; whatever you bind on earth will be bound in Heaven, and whatever you loose on earth will be loosed in Heaven"* (Matt. 16:19).

Authority and power will combine together to create a healing ministry for those who wear the Designer's clothes, as they will get results like Jesus did, for *"all who touched Him were healed"* (Matt. 14:36).

The "Go" of the Gospel

After the Spirit exercises power and authority through the disciples, He will lead those who wear the Designer's clothes into the "Go" of the gospel. They will go and *"preach this message: 'The Kingdom of Heaven is near.' Heal the sick, raise the dead, cleanse those who have leprosy, drive out* demons. *Freely you have received, freely give"* (Matt. 10:7-8). They will "Go" into all the world and preach the good news to all creation.

> *And these signs will accompany those who believe: In My name*
> *they will drive out demons; they will speak in new tongues; they*
> *will pick up snakes with their hands; and when they drink deadly*
> *poison, it will not hurt them at all; they will place their hands on*
> *sick people, and they will get well* (Mark 16:16-18).

Many wearing the Designer's clothes will be sent out to the nations to preach the Gospel of the Kingdom with signs and miracles after they have established foundational ministries in their home city or nation.

Those who wear the Designer's clothes have been given *"the knowledge of the secrets of the Kingdom of God,"* so they will naturally function as trainers and equippers of the army of God (Luke 8:10). They will flow in the gifts of the spirit and the fruit of the Spirit (see Gal. 5:22). They will thus be able to bring others into complete unity, letting the world know that the Father sent Jesus (see John 17:23). Like Jesus, they will also be *"full of joy through the Holy Spirit"* (Luke 10:21). They will have compassion for the sick and heal them all (see Matt. 14:14).

Those who wear the Designer's clothes put on the Lord Jesus Christ; therefore, they belong to God, for *"He who belongs to God hears what God says…"* (John 8:47). So they will easily prophesy for, like Jesus, they will say, *"The words I say to you are not just My own. Rather, it is the Father, living in Me, who is doing His work"* (John 14:10). This is especially true since Joel prophesied that:

> *In the last days, God says, I will pour out My Spirit on all people. Your*
> *sons and daughters will prophesy, your young men will see visions,*
> *your old men will dream dreams* (Acts 2:17-18).

Therefore, all children of God in these days can hear God's voice and prophesy, including those children who wear the Designer's clothes.

Those who wear the Designer's clothes are the disciples who Jesus said would do greater things than He did. They will not only heal, deliver, raise the dead, cast out demons, prophesy, and have character qualities derived from the Holy Spirit's fruits. Those who wear the Designer's clothes will also do far more beyond what their wildest dreams can imagine, for they will see God do amazing things as He works through them (see John 14:12).

Many of those who will wear the Designer's clothes will participate in signs and wonders. They will "rebuke the winds and the waves" and make them completely calm; they will walk on the water; some will be translated and transported by the Spirit of the Lord as Philip was; they will be the children of God who will liberate creation from its bondage to decay and bring it into the glorious freedom of Jesus Christ (see Acts 8:39; Matt. 8:26; 14:25; Rom. 8:20-21). They will know that God raised them up with Christ and seated them with Him in the heavenly realms (see Eph. 2:6). So they will go up to the third heaven and visit with the Lord; they will join Him in His intercession and call down His power onto the earth to bring freedom, life, and the Kingdom of God on other people and creation.

The primary function for those who will wear the Designer's clothes is that they will testify to the resurrection of the Lord Jesus with great power, signs, and miracles (see Acts 4:33).

ACQUIRING THE DESIGNER'S CLOTHES

You acquire the Designer's clothes by first receiving the light of life. This light is only received when someone prays to receive Jesus Christ as their Lord and Savior and asks Him to forgive all his or her sins and to give him or her a new life in Christ. Jesus then gives the believer a deposit of the Holy Spirit, who is the *"light of life"* (John 8:12).

After you have prayed to receive the Lord Jesus Christ as your personal Savior, you are then supposed to follow the Lord's example by being baptized by full immersion in water in the name of the Father, the Son, and the Holy Spirit (see Matt. 28:19). This is an act of obedience, and new believers often fulfill this step by finding a church to belong to, attending baptism classes, and then being baptized in water.

Once you have received the Lord Jesus Christ and you have been baptized in water, then you begin putting on the Designer's clothes. Putting on the Designer's clothes is accomplished by engaging in a regular prayer time I call soaking. I explain how I soak in Appendix A: Soaking. Our culture does not like to wait; however, putting on the Designer's clothes requires the sacrifice of time to wait to be filled. This sacrifice and waiting to be filled are worth it, as there are eternal consequences, but it is counter to our cultural practice to wait or to sacrifice our time for something other than what is on our "to do" list. If you can break out of the cultural constraints and spend the time coming close to God for several hours a day over several months, the rewards will be tremendous. After spending regular extended time in the Spirit's presence, you will begin to manifest some of the functions of those saints who wear the Designer's clothes which are listed in this section.

If you have never prayed to receive the Lord Jesus Christ and you are willing to do that today, just speak the words in the prayer below out loud. Let's pray now.

Prayer to Receive Jesus Christ as Lord and Savior

Lord Jesus Christ, I come to You today to confess my need for You. I understand that You are the only way to the Father, so

I realize that I must ask You for the forgiveness of my sins, for You provide the only way for my sins to be forgiven. So I pray, Lord Jesus, that You would forgive me of all my sins now. (Mention any specific ones that come to mind individually; be open and honest with the Lord. After you have confessed all sins that come to your mind, proceed with the next paragraph of this prayer).

Lord Jesus Christ, I receive Your forgiveness now. Thank You for forgiving my sins. I believe You lived a perfect life, You were without sin, You died on the Cross, You were resurrected three days later, and now You sit at the right side of the Father on Your throne in Heaven. I believe Your blood poured out is powerful and effective to cleanse me from my sins, so please cleanse me now with Your blood. I ask You to sit on the throne of my life. I choose to step down off the throne, and I ask You to reign in my life.

I ask You, Holy Spirit, to fill me, teach me, and be my guide into all truth. For I understand that the truth will set me free. Lord Jesus, I ask You to help me find a group of believers that I can fellowship with, and also help me to read the Bible and learn to walk through life with You. Thank You for my salvation, Lord Jesus. Amen.

If you prayed that prayer, you are now a new creation in Christ. You now will get to learn to grow in your personal relationship with Jesus, and you will do that by reading the Bible, having fellowship with other believers, and by praying and talking with Jesus and soaking in God's presence.

If you prayed this prayer and received Jesus Christ, please send me an e-mail so I can pray for you. My e-mail address is listed at the back of this book.

The Full Armor and the Attributes of Christ's Ministry

The Designer's clothes are spiritual clothes. They are the clothes that Jesus wore. They are the brilliant white light that surrounded Him like a cloud that seers saw in the spirit and that the disciples saw when Jesus was transfigured. The light was always there, surrounding Jesus once He was full of the Holy Spirit and power. That is why people wanted to touch Jesus' clothes—they wanted a touch of the Kingdom of God. Peter and Paul also wore the Designer's clothes, and they released the Kingdom around themselves as well.

The Designer's clothes are a manifestation of the Lord's glory that brings the Kingdom to the earthly realm. When the Kingdom comes, healings, deliverances, miracles, prophetic insights, and signs and wonders occur; and nature will respond to the prophetic decrees, and the creation will be transformed. The realm of Heaven opens up around those who wear the Designer's clothes.

Wearing the Designer's clothes is actually wearing Jesus Christ Himself. As a result, those who wear them live in Jesus and do not continue to practice sin (see 1 John 3:6). They take their sinful nature to the Cross daily and allow Christ to live in them, and as a result, they are protected from the devil's schemes. The sons of God, for whom creation is waiting, will emerge so that creation can be liberated, and they will be wearing the Designer's clothes.

Those who are transformed by the power of God will wear the Designer's clothes and testify to the resurrection of the Lord Jesus with great power, signs, and miracles. They will participate with the angels of God; they will bring in the great end-times harvest. The full armor of God does not really define the fullness of Christ's attributes and functions; therefore, the definition of the Designer's clothes includes those attributes of the full armor of God, but also extends beyond to include all the possible attributes of Jesus Christ's ministry and the ministers of the other disciples who operated in the spiritual gifts.

~

Discussion Questions

1. Discuss how wearing the Designer's clothes entitles you to do everything that Jesus did.

   ☙ What barriers in your thinking do you have with this?

   ☙ What do you have to do to have faith and believe and step out in this promise?

2. Of the things listed in this chapter, discuss:

   ☙ What functions do you have the faith to step into?

   ☙ What things don't you have the faith for yet?

   ☙ What needs to happen for you to acquire the higher faith levels?

3. Make a goal today about how you are going to acquire the Designer's clothes.

   ☙ What time of day will you soak in the Holy Spirit?

   ☙ How much time will you allocate daily?

   ☙ What will you need to give up to accomplish your soaking goals?

PART III

~

THE LAST DAYS' REQUIREMENTS

In Acts 2, Peter says, *"This is what was spoken by the prophet Joel: 'In the last days, God says, I will pour out my Spirit on all people…'"* (Acts 2:16-17). Peter said that almost two thousand years ago when he identified that we were in the last days. The year 2010 according to the Gregorian calendar is the year 5770 in the Hebrew calendar. We do not know when the end will come, for only the Father knows (see Matt. 24:36). Perhaps the last days will culminate some time before we reach the year 6000 on the Hebrew calendar?

Peter says, *"But do not forget this one thing, dear friends: With the Lord a day is like a thousand years, and a thousand years are like a day"* (2 Peter 3:8). Peter makes this statement in the context of speaking about the last days. To what was Peter alluding when he linked a day equal to a thousand years with the Lord? We do not understand how many days are included in the plural form of "the last days." But could it be that the six days of creation from Genesis 1, with the seventh day being a day of rest for God, are a model for the life of the earth? If so, then as Peter said, six days equals six thousand years. So could the final day on earth be sometime on the sixth day, which correlates to the six thousandth year on the Hebrew calendar? Could that be what Peter was saying with, *"A day is like a thousand years"* (2 Peter 3:8)?

If so, will we then rest like God did on the seventh day, which could be during the seven thousandth year on the Hebrew calendar? Our rest in this case would mean our bodily death, but then we go into Heaven to be with God in His heavenly Kingdom. Perhaps the seven thousandth year is the thousand-year reign of those who are blessed to be part of the first resurrection, who are the *"priests of God and of Christ"* and will reign with Him for a thousand years (Rev. 20:6).

The Gospel of the Kingdom is to be preached to all nations, and then the end will come (see Matt. 24:14). Some think that is within reach in the next decade or so, but maybe it will take longer than that, because the Kingdom must be preached and then the end will come. The testimony is not just to be in word only, but when the Kingdom is preached, it will be in power. So I question the outreach that has been done so far in the world, since not very much of it has been done in power. The testimony has been largely missing the Kingdom power quotient, so maybe it will take many more than just a few decades to accomplish this. Maybe the testimony that has been laid so far is only a foundation for the power of God that will be manifested in the coming decades.

The sixth day or six thousandth year on the Hebrew calendar will be reached in 230 years (5770 + 230 = 6000), which is about A.D. 2240 on the Gregorian calendar. So maybe we have at least two centuries to go before the end comes; or maybe the last day will come sooner. We do not know; only the Father knows (see Matt. 24:36). Regardless, we are in the days of the Spirit being poured out, and we are invited to be clothed by the Spirit in these last days. So whether the end comes in a decade or in two hundred years, all believers who follow the Lord Jesus Christ are now stepping into a time of increased responsibility, which I will show from the Scriptures that I address in Part III. The key step is for believers to take hold of their responsibility and be clothed in the glory of God—the Designer's clothes. Then we can preach the Gospel of the Kingdom in the power of the Holy Spirit, and testify to all nations about Jesus Christ.

The physical revelation that I have felt around me that appeared to indicate that I am clothed in the Designer's clothes drove me into the Scriptures to investigate this reality. Reading the Scriptures helped me to awaken to the revelation of Jesus Christ appearing to me, which I describe in the next chapter. These three revelations—my physical sense of the Spirit around me, my search of Scriptures that confirms that the same reality was with other disciples, and the appearance of the Lord Jesus—have all awakened me in my spirit to the need to address the saints and tell them to get dressed in the Designer's clothes. Consequently, the prophetic revelations that I describe in each of the subsequent chapters repeat this same message—to be filled with the Holy Spirit. I am amazed that so many end-times parables point to the theme that believers need to wear the wedding clothes.

I pray that as you read each of the following chapters you will allow the revelation to continue to penetrate deeper into your spirit until you act on it. The devil will try to steal this message about the Kingdom of God—which is the Holy Spirit being in us—from those who do not understand the importance of this message (see Luke 17:21; Matt. 13:19). So rather than viewing the recurring themes of this message in the next few chapters as being redundant, try to allow the recurring themes to underscore the weight and importance of this message—that all believers in this day need to be continually filled by the Spirit.

CHAPTER 10

THE LAST DAY'S EDICT

In the last days, God says, I will pour out My Spirit on all people. Your sons and daughters will prophesy, your young men will see visions, your old men will dream dreams. Even on My servants, both men and women, I will pour out My Spirit in those days, and they will prophesy. I will show wonders in the Heaven above and signs on the earth below, blood and fire and billows of smoke. The sun will be turned to darkness and the moon to blood before the coming of the great and glorious day of the Lord. And everyone who calls on the name of the Lord will be saved (Acts 2:17-21).

They were looking intently up into the sky as He was going, when suddenly two men dressed in white stood beside them. "Men of Galilee," they said, "why do you stand here looking into the sky? This same Jesus, who has been taken from you into Heaven, will come back in the same way you have seen Him go into Heaven" (Acts 1:10-11).

At that time the Son of Man will appear in the sky, and all the nations of the earth will mourn. They will see the Son of Man coming on the clouds of the sky, with power and great glory (Matthew 24:30).

In the summer of 2004, I was sitting in my car one Saturday afternoon at City University in Calgary, Alberta, where I was attending a class. I looked up and saw two oblong clouds floating horizontally against the blue sky, and between them was a gap. In the gap I saw what looked like a man's body, and coming out from that body on either side were waves of undulating white light. The light billowed toward me, but I did not sense that it reached me, as I was more than a thousand meters away. However, my life changed dramatically after that vision. I quit the program at City University, and I began to press into God more. By January of 2005, the Holy Spirit was echoing in my heart this word—"abide, abide, abide."

Then I began to soak in the Holy Spirit's presence to be filled up by the Holy Spirit, after which I was assigned to direct the healing rooms ministry; following that, I went on mission trips and saw Jesus working through me, bringing healings, deliverances, miracles, and prophecy. I also began to have a greater understanding of my identity and birthright in Jesus Christ.

My problem was that I had been asleep most of my life. Even when I saw the vision of Christ in the clouds, the message was warning me in my spirit: *"At that time men will see the Son of Man coming in the clouds..."* (Mark 13:26). He was telling me that He will be coming again soon. I did not take in that vision consciously at that moment, but my life changed dramatically regardless of my being asleep or not. Thanks be to God, for He moved me in the direction I was supposed to go. Ironically, I found out that my call is to wake people up to the time that we are now in, for it's a *kairos* time—a special season, the season we are all to be transformed by the power of God and get dressed in the Designer's clothes.

Although we have all fallen short of the glory of God, we are now called to be transformed into His likeness with ever-increasing glory, which comes from the Lord who is the Spirit (see Rom. 3:23; 2 Cor. 3:18). So it is through the Spirit that we are to attain our ever-increasing glory.

Peter quotes Joel, saying:

> *In the last days, God says, I will pour out My Spirit on all people. Your sons and daughters will prophesy, your young men will see vision, your old men will dream dreams* (Acts 2:17).

What I have noticed is that there are a lot more people who prophesy these days than ever before. Bill Hamon in his book, *Prophets and the Prophetic Movement*, says that the prophets were beginning to be restored to the Protestant church in the 1980s and continuing into the 1990s.[1] Hamon says he has trained over 250,000 people to prophesy. When the Holy Spirit is poured out for people to prophesy, the fruit of that coming to pass is more people prophesying. So with the increasing numbers of prophets and people with the gift of prophesy, it appears that we are approaching the final season of the last of the last days that was first declared to have begun in Acts.

Paul talks about the future glory God will reveal:

> *I consider that our present sufferings are not worth comparing with the glory that will be revealed in us. The creation waits in eager expectation for the Sons of God to be revealed* (Romans 8:18-19).

And he goes on to say the creation itself will be liberated from its bondage to decay and brought into the glorious freedom of the children of God (see Rom. 8:20-21).

The Sons of God are to be revealed:

- They are the ones who will bring the Kingdom of God into the world around them.

- They are the ones who are hungry and thirsty for the things of the Kingdom.

- They are the ones who are willing to wait upon God to be filled with His power, for it is *"'Not by might nor by power, but by My Spirit,' says the Lord Almighty"* (Zech. 4:6).

POSSESSING THE KINGDOM OF GOD

Daniel prophesied about the end times:

> *As I watched, this horn was waging war against the saints and defeating them, until the Ancient of Days came and pronounced judgment in favor of the saints of the Most High, and the time came when they possessed the Kingdom* (Daniel 7:21-22).

Daniel says that the saints of the Most High God will possess the Kingdom. Therefore, saints will finally possess the Kingdom of God, although the saints who preceded them did not possess it. The Kingdom of God in the New Testament is being filled with the Holy Spirit and then the saints are releasing the power of the Holy Spirit and declaring the Kingdom has come (see Luke 11:20; 17:21; Matt. 10:7). So those saints who do not possess the Kingdom will not be operating out of the Spirit's power, but will operate in their own might, power, strength, knowledge, and education. Could it be that the saints who do not possess the Kingdom of God are asleep and blinded by the world system, and as a result, they do not see how they could possess the Kingdom?

To me, that sounds like the Christian church in the western world over the past hundred years, for the vast majority of the church has not possessed the Kingdom, at least not in power. They have their education and theology down, and know how to do inductive and deductive Bible studies, but they do not operate with the power of God or the power of the Holy Spirit—they do not possess Kingdom power. Paul said to the Corinthian church something that should be said to the Spiritless churches of the world today:

> My message and my preaching were not with wise and persuasive words, but with a demonstration of the Spirit's power, so that your faith might not rest on men's wisdom, but on God's power (1 Corinthians 2:4-5).

Paul possessed the Kingdom of God and its power, because the Kingdom of God was within him (see Luke 17:21)

In John 14, Jesus said:

> And I will ask the Father and He will give you another Counselor to be with you forever—the Spirit of truth. The world cannot accept Him, because it neither sees Him nor knows Him. But you know Him, for He lives with you and will be in you. I will not leave you as orphans; I will come to you (John 14:16-18).

Jesus wants to fill us with His Spirit and be with us, but the world cannot receive the Spirit of truth. So, if the church does not flow in the gifts of the Spirit, is it that they have not yet received the filling of the Holy Spirit? Or is it because they are part of the world system and are excluded from the Kingdom of God, so they can't receive the Spirit? These are serious questions, and this is a call to the saints to possess the Kingdom of God, which means coming out of the deception of the world and being filled with the Holy Spirit. This way the saints will receive the Kingdom of God.

The Holy Spirit began to show me the truth about John 14, which says that the world cannot accept the Spirit of truth, *"because it neither sees Him nor knows Him. But you know Him, for He lives with you and will be in you"* (John 14:16). I began to conduct impartation tests with people, pointing my fingers to theirs from a short distance, then I released the Holy Spirit into them. I found that about 70 percent of the people could feel God's presence, regardless of being a believer or not. After people testify to me that they can feel something in whatever way it is manifested to them—like power, electricity, heat, or a cool breeze—I just tell them to leave their hand where it is, and then I pull mine away.

After pulling away, I ask them, "What do you feel now?" True believers continue to feel the same manifestation of the Spirit, but non-believers tell me the power fades away or has left them. This allows me to explain to them that they never really received Jesus into their heart. Many people have come into the Kingdom of God through this test. The point of this story is that some people who thought they were Christians found out that God's Spirit did not stay with them. They had been part of a cultural belief in the idea of Christianity—perhaps they went to church or had fellowship—but they had not really received Jesus into their hearts. They also did not possess one bit of the Kingdom of God (see Rom. 8:16). This is a wake-up call to the church that many people in Christian churches are not true believers, and they need to be converted and discipled and then taught how to be filled with the Holy Spirit.

"For my next book I started taking videos to demonstrate the concepts that I write about in *Surprisingly Supernatural: A Practical Guide to Releasing the Gifts of the Spirit*. I have uploaded the videos to the book's website: "www.transformedbythepowerofgod.com." You can go to the website and view the videos that help illustrate the impartation tests I referred to in the previous paragraph. The video titles are: "Are you a child of God or of the world?" Part 1, "Are you a child of God or of the world?"

Part 2, and "Are you a child of God or of the world?" Part 3. These videos were spontaneous encounters. The videos capture the essence of what was going on and they illustrate the point I want to make about the impartation whether it stays with people or not."

Daniel 7:22 holds a prophecy that in the end times the saints will possess the Kingdom. It surely refers to the people who have *received the filling* of the Holy Spirit and not just *received a nominal portion* of the Spirit. Consequently, I think that possessing the Kingdom really means that the saints are possessed by the Kingdom. Believers who receive the filling and are possessed by the Holy Spirit will have the Kingdom of God overflowing from their lives. Clearly, the people of God, who are the saints in the last days, have the potential to be the sons of God who will bring liberation to people and creation. And clearly they will not walk in that role without being filled with the Holy Spirit, for Jesus said, *"apart from Me you can do nothing"* (John 15:5). So they will be clothed in the glory of God, clothed in Jesus Christ, and they will be wearing the Designer's clothes.

~

Discussion Questions

1. Jesus said, *"I am the Good Shepherd; I know My sheep and My sheep know Me… I have other sheep that are not of this sheep pen. I must bring them also. They too will listen to My voice…"* (John 10:14,16).

   - ✤ Clearly, followers of Jesus can hear His voice. Do you hear His voice? Discuss how you hear Jesus' voice.

   - ✤ Have you had an increased desire to hear from God lately?

2. Do you feel a tug on your spirit telling you that you are supposed to do something big with your life?

   - ✤ Discuss what you think you will do.

   - ✤ Discuss becoming a son of God and liberating creation. Does that idea resonate in your heart?

3. Do you desire to be a saint who possesses the Kingdom?

   - ✤ What will you need to do to possess the Kingdom?

ENDNOTE

1. Bill Hamon, *Prophets and the Prophetic Movement* (Point Washington, FL: Christian International, 1990), 56. Used by permission of Bill Hamon. Note: the prophetic gift has continued to operate in the Orthodox Church for 2000 years.

Chapter 11

What Is a Christian?

Therefore I tell you that the Kingdom of God will be taken away from you and given to a people who will produce its fruit. He who falls on this stone will be broken to pieces, but he on whom it falls will be crushed (Matthew 21:43-44).

Now that I understand that the Holy Father wants to clothe His children in the Designer's clothes, I have a new understanding of what it means to be a Christian. In this chapter, I want to briefly give you my current answer to the question: What is a Christian? There are many variations to that answer, but lately the following Scriptures have shaped my thinking.

Start with Belief

First, we read what Jesus tells us:

For God so loved the world that He gave His one and only Son, that whoever believes in Him shall not perish but have eternal life (John 3:16).

Paul tells us in Romans 10 how we declare what we believe:

> *That if you confess with your mouth, "Jesus is Lord," and believe in your heart that God raised Him from the dead, you will be saved* (Romans 10:9).

The Christian life starts with your belief being expressed through a verbal confession from your heart that Jesus is the Lord. I clarify to people who desire to receive Jesus Christ that they must make their confession with their whole being—including their mind, will, emotions, and spirit—which is what the heart is.

Belief Requires Action

James tells us that if we have faith, we need deeds to prove it (James 2:14). And Jesus tells His followers,

> *All authority in Heaven and on earth has been given to Me. Therefore go and make disciples of all nations, baptizing them in the name of the Father and of the Son and of the Holy Spirit, and teaching them to obey everything I have commanded you...* (Matthew 28:18-20).

If we believe, we are then to be made into disciples, which means being learners. We need to learn to obey everything Jesus commands us to do. Jesus is the Most High God, the Creator of the Universe, and He commands us to do these things. One of the things disciples need to learn is to respond to the Lord's commands. Sometimes our cultural influences have inoculated us from being responsive to other commands; however, a Christian is called to obedience, which means that a Christian learns to obey what the Lord Jesus commands him to do. One special command is that believers need to learn to make disciples of all nations, which implies participating in evangelism and missions. That is the prime focus of disciples—making other disciples and teaching them everything Jesus commanded. What else did Jesus command?

ACTIONS OF FAITH

Jesus also tells us:

Whoever believes and is baptized will be saved… (Mark 16:16).

We are commanded to be baptized. As discussed in this book, baptism is both being baptized in water and baptized in the Holy Spirit. Jesus tells us when believers are baptized they will have these signs:

… In My name they will drive out demons… place their hands on sick people, and they will get well (Mark 16:17-18).

The signs of a believer are to drive out demons and to heal the sick. Jesus is not commanding that here, but He is stating it as a matter of fact that true Christians will see these signs manifested in their lives. If you don't see them in your life, you probably need to have your mind renewed (see Rom. 12:2). Jesus also commands the disciples that when they engage in evangelism and missions they are to:

Heal the sick who are there and tell them, "The Kingdom of God is near you" (Luke 10:9).

And he commands the disciples:

"… As the Father has sent Me, I am sending you." And with that He breathed on them and said, "Receive the Holy Spirit" (John 20:21).

We too are commanded to receive the Holy Spirit, and to go out and drive out demons, heal the sick, and tell them the Kingdom of God is near. That is because Christians are sent out like Jesus was sent out. This is just part of what believers are commanded to do. Paul tells us the Holy Spirit sanctifies the Gentiles (see Rom. 15:16). The Holy Spirit makes us holy, and that pleases our Lord. The Holy Spirit also empowers believers to heal sick people and to drive out demons, which also pleases the Lord if we do those things. The Lord is pleased with fruitfulness in our lives, as He took away the Kingdom from those who were not fruitful:

> *Therefore I tell you that the Kingdom of God will be taken away from you and given to a people who will produce its fruit. He who falls on this stone will be broken to pieces, but he on whom it falls will be crushed* (Matthew 21:43-44).

Clearly the Lord wants His disciples to produce fruit, and if we are not fruitful, He has been known to take away the Kingdom of God. The Kingdom of God is the Holy Spirit, and the Holy Spirit makes us children of God (see Luke 17:21). If it is taken away, we would be disinherited. So believers need to prioritize being fruitful on behalf of the Kingdom of God.

The priority when becoming a believer is to pray to receive Jesus Christ, and then be baptized in water and in the Holy Spirit. Then, believers need to learn how to make disciples, heal the sick, and cast out demons; and then they should take that learning to the nations of the world, as those are the key areas of fruitfulness for the Kingdom of God. This is the short course for obeying the Lord's commands.

Many believers do various acts of faith and love and charity; however, these acts do not mean they are not supposed have the Holy Spirit and the signs of driving out demons and healing the sick in their lives. Those signs follow after all believers. All Christian believers are to see those signs. If you don't see those signs, then you may need your mind to be renewed, or you may need some inner healing to find out what is hindering you from walking in your birthright in Christ. The Lord calls believers to produce the fruit of the Kingdom, which is to manifest love and righteousness and demonstrate the power of God.

However, Scripture implies that the Lord not only wants us to be fruitful, but He also wants us to be broken to pieces. Being broken is to help us manifest more of the Lord's Kingdom character and power, since it will help to produce obedience in us. But this is difficult for many believers to do, as we don't understand His light, and we don't really know what it takes to become a true believer.

THE DIFFICULT JOURNEY OF FAITH

It is very easy to pray and receive Jesus Christ, yet to follow the Lord throughout one's life can be exceedingly difficult. Jesus is the light of men, but many believers still need illumination.

In Him was life, and that life was the light of men. The light shines in the darkness, but the darkness has not understood it (John 1:4).

Many believers may not have understood the light of the Lord fully. The Lord explains that to us in Matthew 7 where He said:

Enter through the narrow gate. For wide is the gate and broad is the road that leads to destruction, and many enter through it. But small is the gate and narrow the road that leads to life, and only a few find it (Matthew 7:13-14).

Jesus tells us that the narrow gate is one gate that only a few believers find, even though it is the gate that leads to life! This makes me question the total emphasis on being saved by grace. Sure, we are saved when we receive Christ and His mercy, but it looks to me as if He wants some fruitfulness in the life of believers once He has saved us. Few find the fruitful life, even though that fruitfulness is also grace. It is the empowering presence of the Lord's Spirit who gives us the power to drive out demons and heal the sick. We still need the ongoing work of grace in our lives to be obedient to the Lord. Another hindrance to fruitfulness that Jesus tell us about is doing His will:

> *Not everyone who says to Me, "Lord, Lord," will enter the Kingdom of Heaven, but only he who does the will of the Father who is in Heaven* (Matthew 7:21).

We can only know the Father's will if we hear His voice. If we do not know how to hear His voice, how can we obey? Believers need to be illuminated by the Lord and need to be able to hear the Father's voice in order to follow His commands. Many believers have never been taught that we need to keep pursing the Lord to know Him and serve Him. Perhaps that is because the greatest commandments are exceedingly difficult to do. The Lord says:

> *Love the Lord your God with all your heart and with all your soul and with all your mind... Love your neighbor as yourself. All the Law and the Prophets hang on these two commandments* (Matthew 22:37,39-40).

These commands are exceedingly difficult to follow because to love the Lord with all our being means we must lose our life:

> *If anyone would come after Me, he must deny himself and take up his cross and follow Me. For whoever wants to save his life will lose it, but whoever loses his life for Me will find it* (Matthew 16:24-25).

Losing our life means that we are to lose our soul—our mind, our will, and our emotions. Many of us are not prepared to lose what has taken years to construct. Besides, after we lose it, the question is unclear, "Who we will become?" Many believers do not even begin to lose their lives. But this is the call for believers to be transformed, and we each can lose our individual life (soul) and replace it with the heart and mind of Christ. We need to become servants of one another and servants of the Lord God, although our pride often does not want to die. Many believers do not want to take up their cross to follow Jesus, but if we are true followers of Jesus, then we are called to deny ourselves and pick up our cross to follow Him. Our spirit may be willing, but our flesh is weak (see Matt. 26:41; Rom. 7:18-23).

Believers need the Holy Spirit. Believers need to listen to the Lord's voice and to the Scriptures and to other believers. Believers need to be transformed by the Holy Spirit, and by receiving inner healing we can assist other believers in this transformation process. The journey of faith is difficult because we are still part of the world, but Jesus said:

> I have revealed You to those whom You gave to Me out of the world. They were Yours; You gave them to Me and they have obeyed Your word (John 17:6).

Believers are supposed to have been taken out of the world, but the difficulty is, "How do we to get the world out of believers?" When believers do not know that our hearts are deceitful above all things, we can't get the world out of our soul (see Jer. 17:9). But true believers are supposed to begin the process of learning how to get the deceit and the world out of our hearts so we can become true followers of Jesus Christ.

When Jesus was addressing the issue of transformation for the rich man, He stated:

> It is easier for a camel to go through the eye of a needle than for a rich man to enter the Kingdom of God (Luke 18:25).

Jesus pointed out that the process of our transformation may be challenging and next to impossible to accomplish, but He also said:

What is impossible with men is possible with God (Luke 18:27).

Our transformation is possible with God, Jesus tells us. That is the grace of God operating not only to save us, but also to transform us. This is what a Christian, who is a learner, will learn to do—to be transformed by the power of God and become a follower of Christ who has lost his life and now lives with Christ and lives for His will. The Lord's primary focal points are to have His disciples know the only True God and Jesus Christ—which means we are to have an intimate relationship together—and also to have His disciples demonstrate the Kingdom of God to all the nations. The result is making more disciples (see John 17:3; Matt. 24:14; 28:19). Intimacy and evangelism are two of the most important keys for believers to center their lives around, because they are the Lord's priorities. The fruit of evangelism comes from being intimately acquainted with the Holy Spirit.

In Chapters Twelve through Sixteen, I will address the end-time parables which are interpreted from the perspective expressed in this chapter. I will also share the revelation that the Lord is making a shift and calls believers to participate in it now. This shift is evident from many of the end-time parables that emphasize that believers must wear the "right clothes" for the wedding banquet. The wedding banquet is at the end of the age. Jesus is telling those believers who live just prior to the wedding banquet—those Christians who are alive during the end-times—that they must be dressed in the Designer's clothes, which is to be clothed in the Lord Jesus Christ Himself. This was not taught to me in the churches or the schools I attended, but I believe it was revelation from the Holy Spirit, who taught me and showed me from the Scriptures the shift in how Christians are to live in the end-times. The Lord wants His Body to wake up and get dressed at this time! (See Revelation 16:15.)

The end-time parables also address the need for believers to truly express love to one another. Again, this is a call to have the Holy Spirit heal us and for believers to use Christian inner healers who can help us in the transformation process. I believe the Lord Jesus Christ wants His disciples to be filled with His Spirit and transformed and then sent out like He was—in the power of the Holy Spirit—so we can demonstrate the Kingdom of God to all the nations of the world. Believers are on various spots along the path of becoming transformed and being anointed followers of Christ, but we can hasten our journey by being filled by the Holy Spirit. Our transformation may seem impossible for us, but it is possible with God when His Holy Spirit is in us and around us (see Luke 18:27; 2 Cor. 3:17-18).

There are more people alive today than at any other time in the history of the world; there are more Muslims being born today than any other group of people in the West. The Lord is impassioned because He does not want anyone to perish, but He wants all who can to come to Him and receive salvation. That is why the believers are called today to be transformed, filled, and then sent out like Jesus was. The end of the age is approaching, when it is time for Christians to become fully alive in Christ, and we get to bring in the harvest.

What Is a Christian?

In my impartation experiences with some Christians, the Holy Spirit did not stay with them. They were not "Christians" from God's perspective or from that of the Scriptures (see John 14:15-18; Rom. 8:14-17). A Christian is a person with belief in Jesus Christ that has been expressed verbally, and the Christian is baptized in water and baptized repeatedly in the Spirit. Being filled with the Spirit of Christ is a hallmark of being a Christian. The Greek word for Christ is *Christos,* which means "anointed" or "Messiah." The word "Christ" was a description of Jesus, not His last name. It meant Jesus was the anointed Messiah. Christians are supposed be like little messiahs and walk upon earth like Jesus did, because they have the Holy Spirit.

A Christian is someone who is a learner and who learns to follow the commands of the Lord, which include driving out demons, healing the sick, hearing the voice of the Father, and obeying what He calls the believer to do. A Christian knows the heart of the Lord is for intimacy. The believer knows the Lord, then grows to learn that the Lord's heart is for the Christian to learn to demonstrate the gifts of the Spirit by driving out demons and healing the sick. Then Christians take the Kingdom of God out to the nations to do evangelism and missions and make more disciples.

The name "Christian" has been watered down and today it has lost its original meaning. But I believe the Lord wants to bring the original meaning back to the word "Christian," which is why He gave me the revelation of the Designer's clothes. When believers put on the Designer's clothes, they are putting on the Lord Jesus Christ, and they walk around their daily life with the Lord Jesus Christ with them. He did tell us He would always be with us *"to the very end of the age"* (Matt. 28:20). When believers wear the Designer's clothes, they are transformed into the Christians that the Lord planned even before creation (see Eph. 2:10). They walk upon the earth obediently doing what the Lord calls them to do, by healing the sick, raising the dead, driving out demons, and preaching the Gospel of the Kingdom, showing that:

> *Salvation is found in no one else, for there is no other name under Heaven given to men by which we must be saved* (Acts 4:12).

From the Scriptures and especially from the end-time parables, I believe the Lord really wants to put the "Christ" back into "Christians." This idea shapes my current brief definition of a Christian. I am unsure if anything less is a real Christian. The Lord implores the Church to wake up! Perhaps we have been asleep to not having Christ within Christians. While there are different levels of progress, disciples are called to make disciples and teach them everything Jesus commanded. I think what I describe here as a Christian is just how ordinary believers are supposed to operate in their daily lives. When seekers do the things Jesus commanded, they become Christians and also become children of God.

Discussion Questions

1. Have you noticed that some Christians do not shine their light and do not act any differently from the nonbelievers in their social group?

   ☙ Why do you think they fail to shine their light?

   ☙ What activity do you think would entail shining one's light as a Christian?

2. Why do you think Jesus taught about the narrow road and that only those who do the will of the Father will enter the Kingdom of Heaven? (See Matthew 7:14,21.)

   ☙ Why would someone tend to ignore reflecting on the verses of Scripture given in this chapter?

   ☙ If we are saved by grace, why do we have to walk on the narrow road?

   ☙ To do the will of the Father requires what response from the believer?

3. Have you understood how to lose your life and how to allow yourself to be broken to pieces?

   ☙ What is the challenge of losing your life?

   ☙ How can you walk in faith and allow the process of losing your life to take place?

- How do our culture's influences, including the influence of our churches, help us to resist losing our life and being broken to pieces?

- Have you ever prayed for the Lord to help you lose your life or be broken? If not, why?

- Did you realize that the Christian's transformation process is grace as well?

4. Have you read the end-time parables and wondered what they were saying to the Church at that time?

    - Have you ever thought about the emphasis of wearing the right clothes to the wedding banquet?

    - Have you ever wondered what the clothes might be?

    - Do you think they might be the Designer's clothes?

5. What do you think of the idea that some Christians may not be "Christians" from God's perspective or from the perspective of the Scriptures?

    - Being a Christian means believing in Jesus and then taking actions of faith and obedience. What are the actions of faith and obedience you have understood before?

    - What actions of faith and obedience are you now aware that you need to do?

    - Being filled with the Holy Spirit puts the "Christ" into Christians. Discuss how important this is for true Christians to understand and then do.

    - Being a Christian means demonstrating the gifts of the Spirit and making other disciples. How fruitful have you been in the past at doing these things?

6. If your fruitfulness has not been abundant, do you think wearing the Designer's clothes will help you become more fruitful?

CHAPTER 12

THE WEDDING BANQUET

Jesus spoke to them again in parables, saying: "The Kingdom of Heaven is like a King who prepared a wedding banquet for His Son. He sent His servants to those who had been invited to the banquet to tell them to come, but they refused to come. Then He sent some more servants and said, 'Tell those who have been invited that I have prepared My dinner: My oxen and fattened cattle have been butchered, and everything is ready. Come to the wedding banquet.' But they paid no attention and went off—one to his field, another to his business. The rest seized his servants, mistreated them and killed them. The King was enraged. He sent His army and destroyed those murderers and burned their city. Then He said to His servants, 'The wedding banquet is ready, but those I invited did not deserve to come. Go to the street corners and invite to the banquet anyone you find.' So the servants went out into the streets and gathered all the people they could find, both good and bad, and the wedding hall was filled with guests. But when the King came in to see the guests, He noticed a man there who was not wearing wedding clothes. 'Friend,' He asked, 'How did you get in here without wedding clothes?' The man was speechless. Then the King told the attendants, 'Tie him hand and foot, and throw him outside, into the darkness, where there will be weeping and gnashing of teeth.' For many are invited, but few are chosen" (Matthew 22:1-14).

In Matthew 22, we read the parable of the wedding banquet, where Jesus says, *"The kingdom of heaven is like a King who prepared a wedding banquet for His Son"* (Matt. 22:1). And He goes on to say that those who were invited to come did not come. These were the Jews who were invited, but they did not come in and receive Jesus and His Spirit. So He had His servants go to the streets and get all the people, both the good and the bad. These people are the Gentiles who came to faith in Jesus Christ, who are invited to the wedding supper of the Bridegroom. We know that the wedding banquet is the banquet at the end of the age.

One of the responses of the people who were invited to the wedding banquet of the Son is that they refused to come (see Matt. 22:3). Another response was that they paid no attention and went off (see Matt. 22:5). Refusal to come and paying no attention indicates that they would not get dressed for the occasion. It also shows that they did not recognize the importance of the occasion—that is, the wedding banquet for the Son. In Revelation, Jesus implores the Church to stay awake until He comes back so they can be ready (see Rev. 16:15). Staying awake is the opposite of refusing to come or not paying attention. You stay awake by coming to receive the Holy Spirit of God, and then you pay attention so you will meet Jesus when He arrives. This is one of the themes of those who are invited to come to the wedding banquet. Those invited to come to the wedding banquet must come to God and know Him by His Spirit, and also remain awake and pay attention to the announcement of the wedding banquet.

POWER TO SHINE

Another theme is found in Matthew 22, which says the King noticed a man not wearing wedding clothes. *"'Friend,' He asked, 'how did you get in here without wedding clothes?' The man was speechless"* (Matt. 22:12). And the King had him cast outside into darkness.

The King called the Gentile believer, "Friend," which I believe means he must have had the light of life, but the King asked about his missing wedding clothes. When I note that the "Friend" must have had the "light of life," I am referring to what Jesus said: *"...Whoever follows Me will... have the light of life"* (John 8:12). And Jesus also said, *"You are the light of the world... let your light shine before men, that they may see your good deeds and praise your Father in Heaven"* (Matt. 5:14,16). A believer who is in a relationship with Jesus receives the light of life and is to shine that light. The shining of the light results from having enough power to shine it outward.

In this parable, I believe the "Friend" had the "light of life," but he did not have the power to shine it during the time of life he was assigned to live on earth. The power to shine the light comes from the Holy Spirit (see Luke 24:49). I believe his lack of power to shine is reflected in this parable because he was not wearing the wedding clothes. Since he was at the end-time wedding banquet and he did not have the wedding clothes—which are the Designer's clothes—he was thrown out into darkness. This is a warning for those of us who live in the end-times: we need to wear the wedding clothes, the Designer's clothes.

Note that the darkness may not be the fires of hell. Choo Thomas' book, *Heaven is so Real,* shares the perspective that Christians outside the gate of the Kingdom walk around in gray clothes, because although they were believers, they did not practice obedience and live a godly life.[1] They are not in hell, but they are not living in the Kingdom of God, for the godly life is having a lamp and shining it outward for others to see. Perhaps this observation of Thomas' is corroborated in Matthew 25, which shows the exclusion of those with only a lamp, but without the oil and the obedience. It says, *"The virgins who* **were ready** *went in with Him to the wedding banquet. And the door was shut. Later others also came, 'Sir! Sir!' they said. 'Open the door for us! But he replied, 'I tell you the truth, I don't know you"* (Matt. 25:10-12). The Scripture does not say they were sent out to eternal punishment; it just tells us the door was shut to those people who **were not ready**. "Ready" in this context means having oil, which means being filled with the Holy Spirit. When you have the oil, you can be led by the Spirit and release the kingdom when directed to do so. In the end-times, if you release the Kingdom, you will enter the Kingdom at the end of the age, but only if you have intimacy with the Lord, and that comes from being a sheep who knows His voice and can obey Him. (See John 10:16; Matthew 7:21.)

The wedding feast is a theme in Scripture; it is the celebration that culminates in the end of the age (see Matt. 22:2; 25:10; Luke 14:16-24; Rev. 19:7). Wedding clothes are mandatory for those who want to sit at the wedding banquet. If you wear the Designer's clothes—which means you are filled with the Holy Spirit to overflowing—you will get into the wedding banquet, for you are in Christ and He is in you. Clothing yourself with Jesus Christ is wearing the wedding clothes (see Rom. 13:14).

I do not know if the requirement in this end-time parable to wear the Designer's clothes is meant for all believers throughout the age, or if it is a requirement only for those who live at the end of the age. When you clothe yourself in Jesus, you clothe yourself in the Spirit, for the Holy Spirit is the Spirit of Jesus Christ (see Phil. 1:19). But if you do not wear the Designer's clothes, as this parable describes, you will either not be let in to the wedding banquet, or—if you are let in and found without your clothes—you will be cast out into darkness (see Matt. 22:13).

As I mentioned in the previous chapter, many churchgoers are not true believers. To repeat, in the end-times, if you are not wearing the wedding clothes—the Designer's clothes—you will either not be invited into the banquet, or if you get in, you will be asked to leave. Therefore, in addition to receiving Jesus as their Lord and Savior, believers also need to be Spirit-filled so they will know the Lord intimately and can demonstrate the Kingdom of God, because this is a crucial mandate for the last-days' Church.

I believe the Designer's clothes are the wardrobe that the last generation who will live on earth must wear. The preceding generations of believers may not have needed to wear the Designer's clothes. Although God may have wanted it, there is no indication in Scripture that it was required. But those who will live in the final generation on earth must wear the Designer's clothes—there is no choice—they must do the exploits of God before Jesus Christ's return. We cannot do the exploits without wearing the Designer's clothes, for it is not in our own power, as Jesus said—we must abide in Him and there will be much fruit; without Him we can do nothing (see John 15:5). The exploits will be in the power of the Holy Spirit. Revelation 17 says:

> *They will make war against the Lamb, but the Lamb will overcome them because He is Lord of lords and King of kings—and with Him will be His called, chosen and faithful followers* (Revelation 17:14).

The end-time army of saints consists of the called, chosen, and faithful followers of Christ. This is not a description of nominal or disobedient believers, but of the true believers who will battle against the hordes from hell with the power of God that is in them and surrounds them.

TIME TO GET DRESSED!

The problem we have is that we do not know who will be the last generation on earth. As I stated in the introduction to Part III, "the last days" are plural (see Acts 2:17), and we do not know if they will last for a decade or for two centuries or longer. So if we are not the last generation, we may not need to wear the Designer's clothes. But if we *are* the last generation, we must wear them. I believe the Lord wants believers to be clothed in His Spirit today, so they can demonstrate the gifts of the Spirit, because our demonstration of the gifts is only possible when we are clothed. And the result will be more believers being clothed in His Spirit tomorrow. The Lord is calling for all believers to demonstrate the life in the Spirit, because the Lord wants to see the number of believers who live life in the Spirit to multiply. So the revelation for today is that it is a *kairos* time, which means it is the season to begin putting on the Designer's clothes. We must be ready, and that means we must wait for the Holy Spirit and be filled, for that is what this *kairos* season is about—coming to God, waiting for the Spirit, and being filled to overflowing with the power of God.

Who wants to gamble and *not* put on the Designer's clothes, and as a result, miss out on the great exploits the Church is called to participate in during these last days? Is the last generation alive today? Well, they may be, so this teaching and revelation needs to get into the hearts of believers so they can all walk out and do the works that God has prepared in advance for them to do (see Eph. 2:10).

This interpretation of the wedding banquet parable shows that we do not want to gamble and *not* be filled with the Holy Spirit—the stakes are too high. Some believers may say, "We have jobs, school, families, hobbies, and television: we protest! We do not have time to wait for the Holy Spirit to fill us!" That may be the perception of some, but I personally do not want to take the chance of *not* being filled with the Holy Spirit and then find out afterwards that I was living as part of the last generation on earth and was expected to manifest the Kingdom of God all around me and bring glory to Jesus. If I do not wear the overflow of the Holy Spirit, that may mean I did not bring the glory to Jesus as I was called to do. If that happens, who knows if I will be invited into the wedding banquet or not?

Jesus has plans for those who live in the end-times to bring in the harvest. Missing out on bringing in that harvest would be rebellious and disobedient. No wonder Matthew 22:13 shows that those people who are without the wedding clothes are kicked out into the darkness. Bringing in the end-time harvest is crucially important for the Lord. Therefore, I want to live as if I am *"crucified with Christ and I no longer live, but Christ lives in me... "* (Gal. 2:20). So for Christ to live in me, I must be continually filled by His Holy Spirit to overflowing. Then Christ will partner with me to do great exploits and build His Kingdom here on earth in these final hours by working through me. So come and join me in doing the great exploits we are invited to do as we build God's Kingdom by putting on the Designer's clothes. I hope to see you at the wedding banquet.

Discussion Questions

1. The danger for believers reading these parables over and over again is that we become dull to what they say.

   ☙ Discuss what impact this parable of the wedding banquet had on you before.

   ☙ Discuss it now in terms of you living in possibly the last generation on earth. How will that new reading of the Scripture change how you will live?

2. The wedding clothes determine if you are in or out of the wedding banquet.

   ☙ What do you think the man was wearing who did not wear the proper wedding clothes?

3. Does this understanding move you to make any changes in your life? Discuss the possible changes.

ENDNOTE

1. Choo Thomas, *Heaven is so Real* (Lake Mary, FL: Charisma House, 2006), 163.

CHAPTER 13

USE YOUR TALENTS

Again, it will be like a man going on a journey, who called His servants and entrusted His property to them. To one He gave five talents of money, to another two talents, and to another one talent, each according to his ability. Then He went on His journey. The man who had received the five talents went at once and put His money to work and gained five more. So also, the one with the two talents gained two more. But the man who had received the one talent went off, dug a hole in the ground and hid his Master's money. After a long time the master of those servants returned and settled accounts with them. The man who had received the five talents brought the other five. "Master," he said, "You entrusted me with five talents. See, I have gained five more." His Master replied, "Well done, good and faithful servant! You have been faithful with a few things; I will put you in charge of many things. Come and share your Master's happiness!" The man with the two talents also came. "Master," he said, "You entrusted me with two talents; see, I have gained two more." His Master replied, "Well done, good and faithful servant!

You have been faithful with a few things; I will put you in charge of many things. Come and share your Master's happiness!" Then the man who had received the one talent came. "Master," he said, "I knew that You are a hard Man, harvesting where You have not sown and gathering where You have not scattered seed. So I was afraid and went out and hid Your talent in the ground. See, here is what belongs to You." His Master replied, "You wicked, lazy servant! So you knew that I harvest where I have not sown and gather where I have not scattered seed? Well then, you should have put My money on deposit with the bankers, so that when I returned I would have received it back with interest. Take the talent from him and give it to the one who has the ten talents. For everyone who has will be given more, and he will have an abundance. Whoever does not have, even what he has will be taken from him. And throw that worthless servant outside, into the darkness, where there will be weeping and gnashing of teeth" (Matthew 25:14-30).

The parable of the talents is from Jesus' collection of teachings in Matthew. In this parable, the Master (Jesus) entrusted His servants with His property and went away. Each servant was given talents according to his ability. Upon His return, the servants were either rewarded and invited to share in the happiness of the Master, or were punished and thrown out into the darkness.

There are many things we can learn from this parable. Its main focus is on the talent, a type of ancient money, which represents our money today. The parable is part of the end-time teachings from God, who told us, *"Remember the Lord your God, for it is He who gives you the ability to produce wealth, and so confirms His covenant..."* (Deut. 8:18). The blood covenant for the forgiveness of sins in Jesus' name is the covenant we live in now (see Matt. 26:28). So the wealth we get is given to believers to help confirm to other people the blood covenant in Jesus' name. The wealth we are given is to benefit the Kingdom of God by expanding missions, evangelism, and mercy ministry, and to be used for caring for the poor, the imprisoned, the widows, the orphans, the aliens, and the sick. While this is an important topic, I want to look at this parable from another angle.

GIFTED

The servants in this parable were entrusted with the owner's property. Psalm 24 says, *"The earth is the Lord's, and everything in it, the world, and all who live in it"* (Ps. 24:1). Just like Adam, the human race is responsible for caring for God's natural world and the people and creatures who live in it. We do this with our money and our wealth, but also with our energy and our spiritual gifts. A talent is defined as money, but in a broader Hebrew context, means anything that a person owns that contributes to their livelihood and wealth.[1] Paul says that if you have the Holy Spirit, He gives life to your mortal body (see Rom. 8:11). So, receiving the Holy Spirit can contribute to a person's livelihood by giving him or her good health.

Because of the multi-billion dollar health-care industry, it is good news when testimonies are shared that tell other people how Jesus Himself is healing bodies today. When people get healed by Jesus, it contributes to their livelihood by giving them better health, and it contributes to their wealth by saving on medical costs. This helps to care for God's property— His people, who are healed physically and spiritually. It also affects many non-believers, who will receive Jesus Christ as their Lord and Savior when they discover Jesus healed them. Then the money saved can be invested in the activities that confirm the covenant that I mentioned earlier.

Since the talents represent things that contribute to a person's livelihood, they can be found in both actual money and in the gifts and fruit of the Holy Spirit. This understanding helps us to see that some servants will use their talents and multiply them, while others will bury their talents and gain nothing. I have been sharing with you that the last-days generations are the people who are required to wear the wardrobe—the Designer's clothes—which means that we can demonstrate the Kingdom of God and show that Jesus is the King of kings and Lord of lords. Therefore, the talents for the last-days generations can include both money and the gifts of the Holy Spirit.

Do you remember in Chapter Eight where I discussed how the Holy Spirit is poured out and God's servants will all prophesy? Since in this time more people are prophesying, I concluded that we are now in the final season of the end-times. Therefore, the following questions are pertinent to all believers of this generation:

- Have you buried your ability to prophesy and to hear God's voice?

- Have you availed yourself of the training and equipping schools that teach people how to operate in the gifts of the Spirit?

- Do you share words of knowledge in public venues with strangers?

- Do you use the other gifts of the Holy Spirit in your life regularly?

- Do you believe Mark 16:18 where Jesus says that believers will lay hands on the sick and they will recover?

- Do you regularly lay hands on sick people and expect them to recover?

- Do you believe Mark 16:17 where Jesus says that believers will drive out demons?

- Do you drive out demons from the oppressed people you encounter?

If you are a believer and you respond with a "No" to any of these questions (except the first one), then you are not using the spiritual talents that God has already given you. You may ask, "What has He given me?" We read in Ephesians that believers have been blessed *"with every spiritual blessing in Christ"* (see Eph. 1:3). Jesus Christ has given us every spiritual blessing. However, you may have buried the spiritual talents you are responsible for using.

"Buried" means that you are not using the talents or the spiritual gifts. Jesus said that if you invest your (spiritual) talents and multiply them, God will give you more, and then you will accelerate in power and authority in the gifts to prophesy, to heal, and to deliver. But if you do not invest and multiply them, God will take away what you already have (see Mark 4:24-25). The gifts you are given to prophesy, to heal, or to deliver will diminish when they are not used, so it is best to obey and use the gifts. Hebrews says, *"But solid food is for the mature, who by constant use have trained themselves to distinguish good from evil"* (Heb. 5:14). The mature put into constant practice their spiritual gifts, so they develop discernment between good and evil. A sign that you are maturing is that you practice the gifts. So be sure to use your talents, especially since they are being given out by the Holy Spirit in this hour.

Life in Christ is all about what Christ has done for us. He lived a perfect life, was without sin, and died so that we could have our sins forgiven. He is our righteousness and He gave us every spiritual blessing. Jesus went to the Father after His resurrection, and He said, *"When the Counselor comes, whom I will send to you from the Father, the Spirit of Truth who goes out from the Father, He will testify about Me. And you also must testify... "* (John 15:26-27).

It is the Holy Spirit Who gives us the fruit and the gifts of the Spirit, and with them we must testify about Jesus. That is a command—the saints must testify about Jesus. We need these spiritual talents, and we need to use them for the purposes God wants. The primary purpose for the spiritual talents is to bring glory to Jesus Christ by testifying about Him in the world. Jesus said, "'... *As the Father has sent me, I am sending you.' And with that He breathed on them and said, 'Receive the Holy Spirit'"* (John 20:21-22).

This is pivotal—Jesus wants us to go as He went. And how is that? He sends us out with the Holy Spirit. He wants us to live in Him, to move in Him, and to represent Him on the earth to all humankind and to all rulers and authorities. In response, we are to live obediently and move in the Spirit as He works with us to take dominion over all creation. But unless we use the talents that God has given us, which are the fruit and gifts of the Holy Spirit, we cannot testify as Jesus wants us to. Remember—without Him, we can do nothing (see John 15:5).

Once again, in this end-time parable the mandate is given that the last generations on earth must use their spiritual talents—the gifts of the Holy Spirit—which have already been given out. Why does God pour out His Spirit in the last days if He does not want His people to use the gifts and fruit of the Spirit? In Acts 2:17, He even says that He pours it out so they will prophesy. Prophecy is one of the spiritual talents that He has given to believers today to help care for His property—the earth and those people and creatures who live in it. So all people need to receive the gift of prophecy and then practice it until there is multiplication.

Multiplication could have at least two results. The people who are prophesied over will know that Jesus knows about their lives. If they are non-believers, they may come to faith in Jesus Christ. If they are believers, they can be encouraged to learn to prophesy themselves. More evangelists and people who can prophesy will be the result of these end-time multiplications of the gift of prophecy. The same result will occur with the other gifts of the Spirit, like healing. Non-believers may come into faith in Jesus when they are healed, and believers will be shown that they can operate in the gifts of healing, too. As a consequence, there will be multiplication of the healing gifts demonstrated by other believers. This is a season for us to be disciplined in the practice of the spiritual gifts, so it results in multiplication and the number of saints who use them will increase. This is a *kairos* season.

POURED OUT

When God pours out His Spirit, we must receive it, and to receive it means to ask to be filled with the Holy Spirit to the point of overflowing. As this overflow occurs, believers will testify about Jesus through demonstrations of the gifts and the fruit of the Spirit. Even the talent to make wealth is a gift from God (see Deut. 8:18). So be wise and use all the talents, both your wealth and your spiritual talents that God has given you in this *kairos* season.

In the past few decades, God has raised up ministries to train the saints through prophetic schools like Christian International Apostolic Prophetic Training classes, Patricia King's Prophetic Evangelism classes, John Paul Jackson's Streams Ministry, Elijah House's School of Prophesy, and Toronto Airport Christian Fellowship's leadership schools, to name a few. Deliverance training has been raised up as well, and Bob and Sharon Parkes teach their Prophetic Generational Deliverance model, Doris Wagner has her courses on deliverance, and Paul Cox teaches discernment and generational deliverance courses. Spokane Healing Rooms are a headquarters for the International Association of Healing Rooms, with over seven hundred healing rooms established in the world. These healing rooms teach local believers to lay hands on the sick so they will recover. Global Awakening in Harrisburg, Pennsylvania, and Bethel Church in Redding, California, both have supernatural schools of ministry and teach a variety of spiritual gifts to their students.

With the influx of these and many other ministries that God has raised up, He appears to be saying, "Church, get ready—this is a *kairos* time! Practice your spiritual gifts, and be ready to march out as My army, the army of God, to demonstrate that Jesus Christ is the King of kings and the Lord of lords. He is alive and reigns in power!" God is calling all believers, telling them that they need to be trained in the things of the Spirit and then instructed and encouraged to practice their spiritual talents.

We should remember Jesus' teaching: "... *With the measure you use, it will be measured to you—and even more. Whoever has will be given more, whoever does not have, even what he has will be taken from him*" (Mark 4:24-25). This verse follows right after Jesus taught about putting your lamp on a stand, not under a bowl (see Mark 4:21-23).When you shine your lamp, the oil ignites and burns. This indicates that Jesus is encouraging us to use the grace and character He has given us and the spiritual talents given to us in the form of gifts and fruit of the Holy Spirit. We shine our lamp from the top of the stand by using these gifts. Here is the message for this hour—do not sleep or delay; it is a *kairos* moment. To use our gifts from the Holy Spirit, we must be filled by the Holy Spirit, and filled continually to overflowing, which means putting on the Designer's clothes and putting into practice the gifts of the Spirit.

~

Discussion Questions

1. How did you view the parable of the talents before reading this book?

    ⚬ What did you think the talents represented?

    ⚬ What implications does it have for your life if the talents speak of the gifts and fruits of the Holy Spirit?

    ⚬ How will you begin using these gifts to testify about Jesus in the coming season?

2. If you are entrusted with God's property, the earth, and those who live in it:

    ⚬ How can you care for God's property?

    ⚬ Is there any new way for you to care for God's property?

3. Have you attended or wanted to attend training in any of the gifts of the Holy Spirit?

    ⚬ Discuss how you began to desire to learn about the gifts.

    ⚬ Discuss whether you have been discouraged from attending.

4. Do you have plans to attend any training in the coming year?

    ⚬ Discuss the training schools that you have heard about or attended.

ENDNOTE

1. Strong, *The Exhaustive Concordance* (G5342). "τάλαντον talanton tal'-an-ton"—Neuter of a presumed derivative of the original form of τλάω: "to bear," equivalent to G5342; a balance (as supporting weights), that is, (by implication) a certain weight (and thence a coin or rather sum of money) or "talent."

Other sources on "talents":

- Bill Long, "Parable of the Talents," Dr. Bill Long, http://www.drbilllong.com/LectionaryIV/Mt25.html (accessed November 16, 2008).

- John E. Dubler, "Parable of the Talents," Parables 14, The Talents, http://www.johndubler.com/Parables_14_WEB_Parable_of_the_Talents.pdf (accessed February 28, 2010).

- John W. Ritenbaugh, "Forerunner Commentary," Bible Tools, Matthew 25:14-21, http://bibletools.org/index.cfm/fuseaction/Bible.show/sVerseID/24023/eVerseID/24039/ (accessed February 28, 2010).

CHAPTER 14

THE SHEEP AND THE GOATS

When the Son of Man comes in His glory, and all the angels with Him, He will sit on His throne in heavenly glory. All the nations will be gathered before Him, and He will separate the people one from another as a shepherd separates the sheep from the goats. He will put the sheep on His right and the goats on His left. Then the King will say to those on His right, "Come, you who are blessed by My Father; take your inheritance, the Kingdom prepared for you since the creation of the world. For I was hungry and you gave Me something to eat, I was thirsty and you gave Me something to drink, I was a stranger and you invited Me in, I needed clothes and you clothed Me, I was sick and you looked after Me, I was in prison and you came to visit Me." Then the righteous will answer Him, "Lord, when did we see You hungry and feed You, or thirsty and give You something to drink? When did we see You a stranger and invite You in, or needing clothes and clothe You? When did we see You sick or in prison and go to visit You?" The King will reply, "I tell the truth, whatever you did for one of the least of these brothers of Mine, you did for Me."

> Then He will say to those on His left, "Depart from Me, you who are cursed, into the eternal fire prepared for the devil and his angels. For I was hungry and you gave Me nothing to eat, I was thirsty and you gave Me nothing to drink, I was a stranger and you did not invite Me in, I needed clothes and you did not clothe Me, I was sick and in prison and you did not look after Me." They also will answer, "Lord, when did we see you hungry or thirsty or a stranger or needing clothes or sick or in prison, and did not help You?" He will reply, "I tell you the truth, whatever you did not do for one of the least of these, you did not do for Me." Then they will go away to eternal punishment, but the righteous to eternal life (Matthew 25:31-46).

The parable of the sheep and the goats is found in Matthew, and this parable complements the preceding parable about the talents, as both parables tell us about the responsibility the people of God have to care for God's property—the earth and the people living in it (see Ps. 24:1). But a full discussion of this parable will not be covered here; I only want to capture the key point. Jesus says that the people are depicted as sheep or goats, and that when you act like a child of God and express the love of God by feeding the hungry, giving drink to the thirsty, taking in the homeless, clothing those needing clothes, caring for the sick, or visiting those imprisoned, then you did it to Jesus Himself. A child of God must act like the Son of God. To be truly human is to act like Jesus did. If we fail to act like Jesus, then we will not do those things that Jesus expects us to do, and if we consistently fail to act like Jesus would want us to act, we may be condemned for it.

This parable is addressed to the believers, not to the non-believers. We might want to review our theological understandings. Yes, we are saved by grace, but how about our lives after we are saved? Yes, all blasphemies and sin will be forgiven, but are we expected to walk out the sanctified and transformed life in Jesus Christ? (See Matt. 12:31.) First John 3:6 says that no one living in Jesus will keep on practicing sin. There is an expectation that if we live in Jesus and He lives in us, then we will not go on practicing habitual sin. In this parable, the habitual sin is to ignore others who need food, drink, clothes, a bed, healing, or a visit while in prison. Those practicing this sin habitually ignore meeting the serious needs of the people who live around them. This is not a comprehensive list of needs that believers ought to respond to, but it is indicative of the audience to whom the servants of the Lord are to minister—the poor, the downtrodden, and those who are in need of justice.

Empathy into Action

Dr. Donald McLean from Montreal, Canada, a neurologist, describes the *neuro-cortex* as a unique part of the brain that is only found in human beings—other mammals do not have it. He says that it gives humans three main characteristics or functions:

- the ability to envision future goals and plans

- the ability to have self-reflection

- the ability to have empathy (feeling what someone else is feeling)[1]

God created healthy human beings to have all three of these brain functions operating in their lives. The neuro-cortex idea helps us to see why Jesus taught the parable of the sheep and the goats. People are to care for others, and if they do not, they do not care for Jesus. There is a connection between having *empathy* and caring for others. If you have empathy, you open yourself up to care for others, for empathy gives the person an understanding of what the other person is feeling and thinking. If the other person is in pain or distress, the *empathetic* believer is able to understand their need and respond in love, helping to care for the other person. This parable is in the last-days section, and linked in context to Matthew 24, where Jesus says, *"Because of the increase of wickedness, the love of most will grow cold"* (Matt. 24:12). Love growing cold may be the result of the empathetic abilities of people being shut down or not consistently operating, or people not being conscious of them at all. It is important for believers to understand that two opposing forces are operating in the world:

- Love is growing cold.

- True believers (sheep) will act like Jesus and care for other people's needs in love.

Two different outcomes occurred in this parable. People either had empathy and acted with compassion, caring for the other person who was in need; or they did not have empathy and failed to care for or act on behalf of the other person.

If a person decides not to meet the need of another person, then he or she will have to ignore the need, stop looking at that person and stop thinking about their need.

But when a healthy human[2] operates with all three of the abilities of the neuro-cortex—*future goals, self-reflection,* and *empathy*—then when that person sees someone else who has a need—for example, thirst— he or she may make a quick series of mental, emotional, and spiritual responses that will help to decide whether he or she can help the other person or not. The person could respond in the following manner:

1. The person first sees or hears about the other person's need.

2. Next, the person responds with *empathy,* and begins to understand and feel the pain of the other person's circumstance.

3. Then, the person assesses his or her own ability through *self-reflection,* and the person accesses his or her own energy,

emotional, physical, practical, and spiritual abilities that he or she has available to meet the other person's need.

- With *self-reflection* the person determines if he or she can meet the need.

- Then the person must decide if he or she wants to meet the need of the other person.

- If the person does not want to meet the other person's need, then the other person is ignored.

- If the person wants to meet the other person's need, then the person goes on to step four below. (Healthy Christians have a spiritual influence here since we are called to care for our neighbors, so we are called to want to help the other person who is in need.)

4. The person responds with *empathy* to the other person's situational need and engages in *self-reflection* where the person tries to determine if he or she has the capacity to help the other person. If the person is a healthy Christian, he or she may also *self-reflect* on the command to "love our neighbor as ourselves," which means the Christian may reflect again with empathy on the person's need and not dwell on their own *self-centered self-reflection* that tells them they can't help (see Matt. 19:21). But the healthy Christian may decide, "Yes, I am able to help, and I want to help." Sometimes the choice to help is an act of faith, since the believer may not have the resources to help. But they know that God supplies all our needs; consequently, they choose to help the other person and take the final step.

5. The person who has *empathy* and has self-reflected and determined that he or she can help and wants to help then begins to feel the release of compassion and love rising up within. Then

that person will move to act and meet the need of the other person who was *thirsty* by giving him or her a drink.

The healthy human being who is a Christian has spiritual values and beliefs that are part of their series of responses. We are to love our enemies, care for our neighbors, lay down our lives for our brothers and sisters, and act as Jesus' hands, arms, and feet by extending His love and Kingdom (see Matt. 5:44; 19:21; 1 John 3:16). We are also to love our neighbor as ourselves (see Matt. 19:19). This last verse is how healthy humans who are Christians are supposed to operate:

- Healthy Christians have empathy so they understand what the other person is going through.

- Healthy Christians have *self-reflection,* which is loving yourself and seeing if you can help without killing yourself or damaging yourself (by being unloving to yourself). Yet there is a tension with *self-reflection* to treat your neighbor who is in need with the same care and respect that you treat yourself. So you are to love them like you love yourself. Sometimes you will be called to lay your life down for your brother and sister and meet their need above your own (see 1 John 3:16).

- Healthy Christians operate with *empathy* and with the emotions of compassion and love, which helps them act in response to the other person's need.

The five steps of the responses mentioned in this chapter would take about three seconds. Whether the person cares for the other person or ignores the need is usually based on a conditioned initial response. This is often due to the emotional wounding that results from one person ignoring another person's need, since the first person is unable feel or see the need well enough to be moved to act in love.

Dr. McLean's research shows that people with emotional wounds lose their ability to have a properly functioning neuro-cortex. The person's emotional wounding frequently inhibits their ability to have empathy for other people's needs. The person with a wounded soul fails to see or understand what another person's need is, and instead that wounded person's self-reflection is focused on their self-centered perspective. They form a bitter judgment in their hearts and they lose the ability to empathize. This type of person is one of the goats in this parable. Though they are believers, because of their wounding they habitually do not have empathy, and they fail to respond to other people's needs with compassion and love. These wounded believers do not act like children of God.

It appears that those believers are condemned in this parable because they habitually did not help the people around them who were in need. They failed to see the needs. This is one of the symptoms of being asleep that Jesus warns about, saying that a person is blessed if he or she stays awake (see Rev. 16:15). But in this kind of sleep, you are asleep to your identity as a believer, for you did not see the need nor respond in love and compassion. Jesus says these believers are the ones who are the goats, because they failed to have empathy and act with compassion toward other people who were in need. The people who were in need were Jesus' brothers and sisters, in whom He lives by His Spirit, which is why He said the goats failed to care for Him.

Empathy is the key to helping a believer relate to the weakened position of others. Empathy helps to register the other person's situation in the believer's consciousness. The ability to self-reflect operates within the believer as he looks at his own desires and his own ability to help. But the believer also reflects on the call to love our neighbor as ourselves, which helps to move the believer's heart to act in love.

HEALING THE BROKEN

We are awesome and wonderfully made by God, who has made healthy individuals to have minds and emotions with the capacity to act upon their Godly beliefs and respond positively to the command to love. But not all believers are healthy; many have been wounded emotionally, mentally, and physically many times in their lives. This is the devil's work—to tempt the wounded—which destroys people's *empathy* so they are not able to move with compassion on behalf of other people's needs. The devil comes to *"steal, kill and destroy"* the lives and identities of as many believers as possible (see John 10:10). He has tried to inflict pain and mental and emotional wounding on many young children who never get the necessary healing for their souls. This is especially true as the devil brought into many cultures in the world the lie that emotions are not to be shown, but instead should be buried. This lie has resulted in buried pain and wounding and results in lack of inspiration to act on behalf of others. These wounds leak out through injured peoples' emotions and may result in physical illnesses. These wounds also lead to toxic behaviors later in life and continue to impact the next generation. The enemy has destroyed many people, but there are God-given solutions.

Two remedies will help us to act in the way God requires true believers to act, and both remedies involve the power of the Holy Spirit. The first is being filled with the Holy Spirit, as the Spirit not only heals us but gives us the fruit of the Spirit, which helps us to have empathy, love, and compassion that we can then give away to other people. The second remedy is inner healing, which is a Spirit-led prayer ministry that helps to heal wounded souls.

In the first Holy Spirit remedy, we are filled with the Holy Spirit and given the fruit of the Spirit, and then we begin to experience a continual outflow of the fruit—love, joy, peace, patience, kindness, gentleness, and self-control. When they flow out of us, we begin to interact with other people as Christ intends for us to act (see Gal. 5:22). We become His eyes, arms, and feet. We can touch others with God's love as He pours the fruit of the Spirit through us. Again, we need to see that we cannot love well on our own—we must be filled with the Holy Spirit and live the life in Christ as we walk in Him and in His love.

The second Holy Spirit remedy is inner healing, which is a spiritual prayer ministry that helps people to be transformed and sanctified. Unlike secular counseling, inner healing deals with sin issues and takes the sin to the Cross. It also uses prayer to break bondages, bitter root judgments, expectations, curses, generational curses, and demonic structures. Inner healing is needed by all believers, and it is needed on a regular basis no matter what your background. In Appendix E, I have listed a number of the inner healing ministries that help believers walk into their birthright and be conformed to the image of Christ Jesus.

Being filled with the Spirit until we are transformed by the power of God and put on the Designer's clothes is a call to love the people in the world and the world itself. If we do not get free from the wounding from our past, we will not be able to love well.

So the parable of the sheep and goats is about believers in the endtimes whom satan tried to wound in an attempt to *"steal, kill and destroy"* their birthright in Christ and their emotional and physical life (John 10:10). But God intercedes for us and turns all things *"for the good of those who love Him"* (Rom. 8:28). So God has not only raised up ministries in the last couple of decades to train believers in the supernatural gifts of the Holy Spirit, but He has also raised up ministries over the same period to help free the wounded hearts of believers through inner healing prayer ministries. This *kairos* season is for believers not only to get filled up with the Holy Spirit and transformed by the power of God so we learn to put on the Designer's clothes, but also to receive inner healing for ourselves so we can learn to pour out God's love from our hearts.

Please see Appendix E for a brief list of some of the ministries that offer inner healing for believers.

~

Discussion Questions

1. Discuss what happens in your heart when:

   - A person with a need is near you. Do you recognize it or not?

   - You see a person with a need. After you see it, what happens next? Do you always ignore the need? Do you always care for the need?

   - When you see a person with a need, do you ask the Lord what is on His heart? Do you ask if you are supposed to care for the need?

2. Do you know of any inner healing ministries in your area?

   - Have you yourself gone for inner healing?

   - Do you feel impeded from your birthright in Christ? Ask the Lord in prayer about getting inner healing prayer ministry for yourself.

3. Look at the list of the fruit of the spirit as listed in Galatians 5:22-23 and discuss:

   - What fruit do you exhibit in your character?

   - What fruit are missing from your character?

   - Pray and ask the Holy Spirit to come and fill you with His fruit.

ENDNOTES

1. Lori H. Gordon, *PAIRS Semester Handbook* (Weston, FL: PAIRS International, 1999).

2. Healthy Human Defined: Due to the findings of Dr. McLean that the neuro-cortex in human beings has the ability to 1. access future plans and visions; 2. to self-reflect; and 3. to have empathy, and from a Christian perspective, we know that God created man, so these abilities are from God's design. So a healthy human being is not a subjective judgment, but it is an assessment of the natural abilities that God created in human beings. If those abilities are functioning, there is good health, if they do not function, there is ill health.

   The parable of the sheep and the goats shows that God intends true believers to act on behalf of the downtrodden, and if we do not do that we are not walking out God's call on our life. The inability to have empathy for other people's circumstances is crucial to walk out as God intended His children to walk.

CHAPTER 15

THE END-TIME WARDROBE

The man and his wife were both naked, and they felt no shame (Genesis 2:25).

... he ate it. Then the eyes of both of them were opened, and they realized they were naked... (Genesis 3:6-7).

Behold, I come like a thief! Blessed is he who stays awake and keeps his clothes with him, so that he may not go naked and be shamefully exposed (Revelation 16:15).

I believe the Holy Spirit has led me through Scriptures that alert the last-days Church of the need to be transformed by the power of God and get dressed in the Designer's clothes. This is not a choice—at least not for those who will be the last generation to live on the earth. It is actually a requirement. I do not want to imply that Jesus' return will happen tomorrow, especially if it causes the Body of Christ to forego putting on the Designer's clothes and *not* go out demonstrating the Kingdom of God throughout their relational networks and beyond. The last-days Church will need time to equip and train the Body of Christ to do the works that God has planned in advance for them to do (see Eph. 2:10). But the sooner we get dressed in the Designer's clothes, the sooner we may hasten the return of Christ, which may be in the next decade or in the next two centuries. We just need to get on with wearing God's divine attire. So let's look at some of the Scriptures that imply this.

Be Ready

Behold, I come like a thief! Blessed is he who stays awake and keeps his clothes with him, so that he may not go naked and be shamefully exposed (Revelation 16:15).

In an earlier discussion in Chapter Five, I shared my belief that Adam and Eve were clothed like Jesus was—in a brilliant light. But when they sinned and ate the fruit, the brilliant light disappeared from around them. This resulted in their realization that they were naked and in shame (see Gen. 3:7). In the verse above, Jesus is saying that when He comes back we need our clothes with us, and Jesus echoes this phrase: "... *So they will not go naked and be shamefully exposed*" (Rev. 16:15). These are the same words found in Genesis 2:25 and Genesis 3:7, where Adam and Eve were naked and shamefully exposed as they lost their Designer's clothes.

When Jesus says, "*Blessed is he who... keeps his clothes with him,*" He is not telling the end-time believers that they have to wear their designer clothes, which are the clothes they might buy in a shopping mall so they can cover their bodies (see Rev. 16:15). Nor is He warning believers not to sunbathe without clothes on, or not to take a shower naked—no. I believe Jesus is talking about how the end-time believers must be dressed in the Designer's clothes—clothed in the glory of God.

The Designer's clothes are the end-time wardrobe. I believe Jesus is referring to the clothes in Revelation 16:15, and they are the same spiritual clothes that Paul refers to when he says to *"put on the armor of light,"* and *"clothe yourselves with the Lord Jesus Christ"* (Rom. 13:12,14). They are the same spiritual clothes that Jesus told His disciples about when He said, *"... Stay in the city until you have been clothed with power from on high"* (Luke 24:49). All these Scriptures summarize this book's revelation that we need to put on the Designer's clothes. This reality—wearing the Designer's clothes—will continue to be reinforced in the next chapter.

In Revelation 16:15, the clothes are supposed to keep the person from being naked and shamefully exposed. When Jesus' glory covers us, His righteousness covers us and our sins are cleansed and wiped away. We have no shame or condemnation in Christ Jesus (see Rom. 8:1). God wants to clothe us so we are not naked and ashamed, but are surrounded in bright lights that reflect His glory and power. Not only does His righteousness cover us, but His character and His fruit transform our lives.

Another end-time message found in Revelation 16:15 is that a person is blessed if he or she stays awake. There is a tendency for people, even the elect—those who God calls to be His children—to fall asleep. But Jesus exhorts us to stay awake. My own testimony is that I have been asleep for decades. And when Jesus appeared in the clouds in that vision I described in Chapter Eight, I did not consciously see Him or recognize Him. I was asleep! I thank God that He called me and woke me up. We all need to wake up and get clothed in His glory. This book is sounding an alarm for us in the Church to change our old ways of thinking and renew our minds (see Rom. 12:2). We all need to be filled with the Holy Spirit in this *kairos* season.

Notice that He said in Revelation 16:15 that He is coming like a thief. He is coming when we do not even expect Him to come. Maybe He will come tonight—are you ready? Are you awake? Are you clothed? The next chapter gives even more evidence behind this message that we need to be awake and be clothed in God's glory, which is the Designer's clothes.

~

Discussion Questions

1. Discuss if you have or have not felt in a bit of a daze about pursuing the Kingdom of God and your relationship with God.

   ◦ Do you feel like you are asleep?

   ◦ Do you feel as if you are waking up?

   ◦ How do you plan on being awake in the coming season?

2. Again, we are confronted with the issue of clothes.

   ◦ Do you believe you are called to have a dangerous shadow like Peter's? (See Acts 5:15).

3. Do you feel in your spirit that the clothes you are going to wear are going to help you demonstrate the Kingdom of God and power wherever you go?

Chapter 16

The Ten Virgins

At that time the Kingdom of Heaven will be like ten virgins who took their lamps and went out to meet the Bridegroom. Five of them were foolish and five were wise. The foolish ones took their lamps but did not take any oil with them. The wise, however, took oil in jars along with their lamps. The Bridegroom was a long time in coming, and they all became drowsy and fell asleep. At midnight the cry rang out: "Here's the Bridegroom! Come out to meet Him!" Then all the virgins woke up and trimmed their lamps. The foolish ones said to the wise, "Give us some of your oil; our lamps are going out." "No," they replied, "there may not be enough for both us and you. Instead, go to those who sell oil and buy some for yourselves." But while they were on their way to buy oil, the Bridegroom arrived. The virgins who were ready went in with Him to the wedding banquet. And the door was shut. Later the others also came. "Sir! Sir!" they said. "Open the door for us!" But He replied, "I tell you the truth, I don't know you." Therefore keep watch, because you do not know the day or the hour (Matthew 25:1-13).

Jesus says, *"At that time the Kingdom of Heaven will be like ten virgins..."* (Matt. 25:1). What time is Jesus referring to? Well, Jesus was talking to His disciples earlier when His disciples asked, *"...When will this happen, and what will be the sign of Your coming and the end of the age?"* (Matt. 24:3). Therefore, we see the "time" that Matthew 25:1 is referring to is the end of the age or the last days. Jesus uses this parable to teach us about the end-time Church and show us that we will have the cross-section of believers in the Church who are represented by the ten virgins in this parable.

We read that both the wise and the foolish virgins have lamps (see Matt. 25:1-3). Remember Jesus' statement when He said, *"...I am the light of the world. Whoever follows Me will never walk in darkness, but will have the light of life"* (John 8:12). In Matthew, He said, *"You are the light of the world..."* (Matt. 5:14). Jesus said in Luke 12 that believers need to *"Be dressed ready for service and keep your lamps burning"* (Luke 12:35). Proverbs 20 tells us, *"The lamp of the Lord searches the spirit of a man..."* (Prov. 20:27). So the lamp the virgins carry is the evidence that they have received Jesus Christ and are His followers.

The lamp is the light of life which Jesus gives to those who put faith in Him. We receive a light or lamp to identify us with our God: *"God is light; in Him there is no darkness at all"* (1 John 1:5). And *"Every good and perfect gift is from above, coming down from the Father of the heavenly lights"* (James 1:17). We receive a lamp or light to reflect that we are God's children—it is part of our conformity to the likeness of Christ.

LAMP BEARERS

In Matthew 25 we read about the difference between the wise and the foolish virgins. The wise took oil in their jars along with their lamps so they could keep their lamps burning, but the foolish did not take any oil with them. What is the oil? Oil in Scripture symbolizes the Holy Spirit.

For example, James tells us to have the elders anoint the sick person with oil (see James 5:14). The oil does not heal, but the power of the Holy Spirit does the healing. So in this verse in James, the oil represents the Holy Spirit.

Another example is found in Hebrews: *"I will be His Father, and He will be my Son"* (Heb. 1:5). This is the heavenly Father speaking about Jesus, His Son. It continues that the Father will be *"... anointing You with the oil of joy"* (Heb. 1:9). The Father anoints Jesus with the oil of joy. A fruit of the Spirit is joy, so here again oil symbolizes the Holy Spirit (see Gal. 5:22).

When Jesus read His mandate, He said, *"The Spirit of the Lord is on Me, because He has anointed Me..."* (Luke 4:18). The Father anointed Jesus with the oil of the Holy Spirit. It is noteworthy that Jesus was *"full of the Holy Spirit,"* and then He returned *"in the power of the Spirit"* (Luke 4:1,14). It was only after the Father anointed Jesus in the power of the Spirit that Jesus walked into the birthright for His life. Jesus' oil jar was full, so He walked out in power, demonstrating healings, deliverance, miracles, and prophecy. Being full of the oil of the Holy Spirit was the key that allowed Jesus to walk out in His birthright.

In the parable of the ten virgins, the wise virgins have their jars full of oil. This implies that they are filled with the Holy Spirit. So the wise have the light of life—their lamp, and the oil for their lamp—the Holy Spirit. The foolish only have the lamp, but no oil or only a little bit of the Holy Spirit.

Matthew says, *"The Bridegroom was a long time coming, and they all became drowsy and fell asleep"* (Matt. 25:5). This is Jesus telling us about the end-time church, and I believe He is saying that *the whole Church has fallen asleep!* This idea is echoed in Revelation 16:15, where He says that you are blessed if you stay awake. We need to be diligent, Church, and wake up to receive our blessing. To wake up is to be alert—being awake to what is important as well as doing it. The Church needs to wake up to receive its blessing! The Church needs to wake up and understand its responsibility and its commissioning in this hour!

In Chapter Twelve, I spoke about the talents—the gifts and fruit of the Holy Spirit—and the requirement to use these spiritual talents that God has given you for Kingdom purposes. We need to wake up to the Kingdom purposes and the spiritual talents—the gifts of the Holy Spirit that He has already given us!

In Chapter Thirteen, I spoke about the sheep and goats; the sheep had awakened to the Lord's empathy and compassion, and they saw the needs of those around them and met those needs. Jesus said they were caring for Him when those needs were met. So we need to wake up to the Kingdom purposes and to the inner healing that we need, so we will be equipped to walk out in the love God wants to pour through us and into others.

In Chapter Fourteen, I spoke about the end-time wardrobe believers need to be wearing. Revelation 16:15 says you are blessed if you are awake and have clothes on, so we need to wake up and fill up our oil jars with the anointing of the Holy Spirit and the power of God, and be clothed with the Designer's clothes.

The blessing from Revelation 16:15 is threefold:

1. We are blessed when we wake up to the purposes and spiritual talents that God has given us for this life.

2. We are blessed when the love of God heals our wounded hearts; then His love can flow out of our lives to others in need.

3. We are blessed when we have been filled with the Holy Spirit; then we will be wearing the Designer's clothes. We know that

the Designer's clothes are Jesus Christ Himself. He said He is with us always, so He will partner with us as we walk out and demonstrate the Kingdom of God in our relational networks (see Matt. 28:20).

The other telling issue for the Church today is that there may be the foolish ones who are without oil for their lamps. This is the clarion call to the Protestant church and the Roman Catholic church and any other denomination that has evangelized believers and has told them that when they received Christ in the conversion experience there was nothing more that they needed to receive from the Holy Spirit.

That initial conversion filling was only one filling, but Peter and the other disciples had at least three or four successive fillings. In Luke 4, Jesus went from being filled with the Spirit to returning in the power of the Holy Spirit. Jesus also had more than one filling. So the teaching, "The initial conversion filling of the Holy Spirit is all that is needed," is a lie from the enemy who has deeply infiltrated this error into the mainline Christian churches. Yes, the new believer receives the lamp and some oil, but the new believer does not have the quantity of oil which is the quantity of the Holy Spirit that Scripture clearly calls for us to have.

We have seen examples in the Scripture of the first disciples who performed signs and wonders, and those examples are not for our entertainment pleasure—no! We are to view them as examples of what we are called to do. We can have a shadow like Peter's that healed people, and we can have napkins and aprons like Paul's that did the same. These saints modeled for us how we are supposed to walk—full of the Spirit and faith. Paul's teaching in Ephesians 5:18 indicates that disciples are to be continually filled with the Holy Spirit. Scripture commands the believers to be continually filled, but that teaching has been suppressed in the church because the enemy does not want believers like you and me to walk out in the power of the Holy Spirit and demonstrate that Jesus is the Son of God and the King of kings and reigns from on high. No, the enemy is battling all he can to stop any and all demonstrations of the power of God. The enemy is happy if people have the lamp, as long as they don't get any oil. He can spot them spiritually, and then he deceives them with distractions so the believers will never walk out in the power of the Holy Spirit. That's why he has deceived the majority of believers in churches, lulling them to be content to be Christian in name, but not in power.

The enemy has deceived believers, and unfortunately many of those believers will be counted as the foolish virgins. I want to acknowledge that it is only by the grace of God that I was awakened and taught to be filled with the Holy Spirit. I am not any better than anyone else, but I am desperately hungry and thirsty for more of God and for all that He has for me.

> *Come, all you who are thirsty, come to the waters; and you who have no money, come, buy and eat! Come, buy wine and milk without money and without cost* (Isaiah 55:1).

Here we see God offer to the thirsty the Holy Spirit—symbolized by the waters, the wine, and the milk—so the thirsty will get their fill. They can buy it without monetary cost. Everyone who asks will receive the Holy Spirit.

But the foolish had to go and buy oil. The foolish either did not know it was without cost—except for the cost of spending their time to wait to be filled—or else they were too busy doing other things and they were not paying attention, so they were distracted from coming to God and waiting to be filled with the Spirit. The foolish are influenced by the secular culture and its values. They spend their time and money for things other than what the Gospel calls Christians to be and to do. However, there is a cost for the oil—you have to "come" and "wait" to be filled (see Isa. 55:1; Acts 1:4). So the wise virgins practiced coming to God and waiting for the Holy Spirit to fill them. The foolish failed to come to God and failed to wait for the filling of the Holy Spirit, so when the Bridegroom came they were not dressed in the bridal clothes; consequently, they missed entering into the wedding banquet.

WAIT

In our microwave culture, we have been trained to disdain having to wait. We have also been trained that we can do it on our own. Maybe the foolish virgins have been asleep too long in their own ways of thinking? We are told, *"'For My thoughts are not your thoughts, neither are My ways your ways,' declares the Lord"* (Isa. 55:8). We may need to have our own thoughts transformed.

Our culture has influenced us to be busy with our own lives, our careers, our hobbies, and our "ministry," but the Scripture tells us, *"... You have forsaken your first love"* (Rev. 2:4). Laodicea's church was only lukewarm (see Rev. 3:16). Being lukewarm is kind of like falling asleep, but being filled with the Holy Spirit and the fire of God makes you hot for God. The Laodicean church is thought by some scholars to be a prophetic message about the Church in the last days. The Laodicean church thought they were rich, but God says they were naked (see Rev. 3:17). These two traits speak to the Church of the western world—we think we are rich, but we do not know we are naked. Again, I believe that God is referring to nakedness in relation to not wearing the Designer's clothes— the glory of God that is supposed to be around all true believers in the end-times. We are now in the end-times, although I do not know when the end will come; regardless, we are supposed to cover our nakedness with the glory of God, and we do that by coming to God, waiting for the Holy Spirit until there is an overflow of the Spirit of God that results in us being clothed in the Designer's clothes.

The virgins in Matthew depict a cross-section of the Body of Christ in the end-times—some are believers who are without the oil of the Holy Spirit and some are believers with oil. God desires that there be no foolish virgins in the end-time Church. He clearly warns the end-time Church to be filled with oil or be left out of the wedding banquet and sent into the darkness.

In Chapter Four, I wrote about the flow of the Holy Spirit out of my hands and fingers. I believe that this may be related to Jesus' teaching when He said, *"… If anyone is thirsty, let him come to Me and drink. Whoever believes in Me, as the Scripture has said, streams of living water will flow from within him"* (John 7:37-38). Notice He says first, *"come to Me and drink."* What do we drink? We drink the living water, which is the Holy Spirit, and since you need no money and it is without cost, you drink until you are filled with the Holy Spirit. We are to believe in Jesus according to the Scriptures, not according to some New Age view of Jesus. But when we really see Him as the Firstborn of Creation, the Son of God, the Creator of the universe, the Lamb of God, the Lord of Hosts, the Glory of God, the Wonderful Counselor, and the Everlasting Father, then we will begin to see Jesus for who He really is, and then His Spirit flows through us like streams of living water.

These streams flow from within us. The Holy Spirit flows out from me and comes out of my hands like a river—sometimes it is vibrations, sometimes it is energy, sometimes it is a cool breeze, and sometimes it is fire. The river that flows from the throne of the Ancient of Days as described in Daniel has fire in it (see Dan. 7:10). I do not control how the river flows out of me, but when I ask God to release different manifestations, He frequently responds and releases the manifestation that I requested.

The point here is that I often impart to people gifts of the Holy Spirit, and sometimes the Holy Spirit just fills them up through me with what

He has for them. It is quite fun because some people get drunk in the Spirit or they feel the Holy Spirit from the tips of their toes to the top of their head, and some get healed by the impartation of the Holy Spirit. (See Appendix C: Marcio and Naura's testimony.) I am merely God's service station attendant, giving them a top-up on their oil, but the end-time Church is supposed to be full of oil. The wise virgins depict a portion of the end-time Church who have the oil for their lamps because they have soaked up the Holy Spirit ahead of time. Believers like me, who are filled with the Holy Spirit, will not be able to fill the other believers for long. Other believers need to get oil for themselves, for when the Bridegroom comes, the wise virgins will not be giving out any more oil top-ups.

The lamps must shine. We are to demonstrate the Kingdom of God in and around our relational networks.

> As you go, preach this message: "The Kingdom of Heaven is near." Heal the sick, raise the dead, cleanse those who have leprosy, drive out demons. Freely you have received, freely give" (Matthew 10:7-8).

So as we go around our relational networks, demonstrating the Kingdom of Heaven by healing, deliverance, et cetera, we fulfill the mandate of the end-time Church by revealing that Jesus Christ is alive and well and is the Lord of Heaven and earth. When we are full of oil, we can do those demonstrations. It is no longer that we merely use wise and persuasive words to convince people of Christ's deity, but the call now is for all believers to demonstrate it through the Spirit's power.

The foolish virgins asked the wise virgins to "Give us some of your oil; our lamps are going out" (Matt. 25:8). But the wise virgins said, "No, get your own." While the foolish virgins went to get their own oil, the Bridegroom came; the wise virgins with the oil were ready, and "went in with Him to the wedding banquet. And the door was shut" (Matt. 25:10).

Did you get that? The door was shut! I believe Jesus is clearly telling us that in the end-time generation, only those believers with lamps and oil are considered the Bride of Christ. They are the ones He welcomes into the wedding banquet. He will tell the others, those without the supply of oil that they were supposed to have, those who are not filled with the Holy Spirit, *"I tell you the truth, I don't know you"* (Matt. 25:12). Some people rest after receiving Christ once, and count on always being saved and going to Heaven, but perhaps that is not what is described in this end-time parable.

In Chapter Three, I wrote about how, as I was learning to be filled with the Holy Spirit, I came to Jesus and waited and loved Him by spending time in His presence. That is the way we build our personal rapport with Jesus. As we make time to be with Him, He knows us on an intimate level. As we love Him, we align with His will, so when He asks us to do something, we respond in obedience. He begins to trusts us with more, and He knows we love him. We also learn to know Him and know His ways. But to the ones who are without oil, He says, *"I don't know you."*

These people had the lamp! They were believers, but were they led by the Spirit? Did they surrender their lives? Did they get filled with the Holy Spirit? When we are led by the Spirit, we have surrendered our lives and have purposefully spent time trying to know God; then we become known by Him as a willingly obedient child. If we do not do those things, we have no intimacy. I implore you to learn to be filled by the Spirit and to grow in intimacy with our loving Lord. It is the best choice you will make, for you were called to be born at this time. Therefore, God must have planned something very special for you to do. But you will only find out if you pursue Him and His Holy Spirit.

Jesus concludes this parable with the statement: *"Therefore keep watch, because you do not know the day or the hour"* (Matt. 25:13). Keeping watch means not only waking up, but also paying attention to the signals that indicate the time is nigh. Therefore, you need your clothes with you, so you need to take the time now and be clothed in the Designer's clothes. I have pointed out in this book again and again the fact that God wants us, His children, to be clothed in the Holy Spirit. So keeping watch in the end-times means watching the time you spend doing other things that distract you, because you will have only a limited time to be filled with the Holy Spirit, and then only a limited time to go out and demonstrate who Jesus is to the world around you. If you do not wake up, get filled with the Holy Spirit, and demonstrate Him in these end-times, you may be locked out of the wedding banquet.

Please understand that having read this book makes you accountable to and responsible for the message contained in it—the end-time Body of Christ is the Bride of Christ who must wear the Designer's clothes, the glory of God, the brilliant light around us if we are to enter into the wedding banquet.

~

Discussion Questions

1. Discuss who you think you are today—a wise virgin or a foolish virgin?

   ~ How do you know if you are awake?

   ~ How do you know if you have a lamp?

   ~ How do you know if you have enough oil?

   ~ In the last week, how have you demonstrated that you have enough oil?

2. Have you been deceived by the lie of the enemy that you received all of the Holy Spirit when you were converted?

   ~ If so, confess and ask for forgiveness.

3. How are you inspired to take this message home with you?

   ~ Will you implement time to come to God and wait for the Holy Spirit?

   ~ Are you willing to share the ideas in this message with other believers in your relational network?

   ~ How are you willing to go and demonstrate the Kingdom of God in your life?

CHAPTER 17

FOR SUCH A TIME AS THIS

Esther also was taken to the king's palace and entrusted to Hegai, who had charge of the harem. The girl pleased him and won his favor. Immediately he provided her with her beauty treatments and special food. He assigned to her seven maids selected from the king's palace and moved her and her maids into the best place in the harem (Esther 2:8-9).

Before a girl's turn came to go in to King Xerxes, she had to complete twelve months of beauty treatments prescribed for the women, six months with oil of myrrh and six with perfumes and cosmetics (Esther 2:12).

Now the king was attracted to Esther more than to any of the other women, and she won his favor and approval more than any of the other virgins. So he set a royal crown on her head and made her queen instead of Vashti (Esther 2:17).

When Esther's words were reported to Mordecai, he sent back this answer: "Do not think that because you are in the king's house you alone of all the Jews will escape. For if you remain silent at this time, relief and deliverance for the Jews will arise from another place, but you and your father's family will perish. And who knows but that you have come to royal position for such a time as this?" (Esther 4:12-14)

Later I passed by, and when I looked at you and saw you were old enough for love, I spread the corner of my garment over you and covered your nakedness. I gave you a solemn oath and entered into a covenant with you, declares the Sovereign Lord, and you became mine. I bathed you with water and washed the blood from you and put ointments on you. I clothed you with an embroidered dress and put leather sandals on you. I dressed you in fine linen and covered you with costly garments. I adorned you with jewelry: I put bracelets on your arms and a necklace around your neck, and I put a ring on your nose, earrings on your ears and a beautiful crown on you head. So you were adorned with gold and silver; your clothes were of fine linen and costly fabric and embroidered cloth. Your food was fine flour, honey and olive oil. You became very beautiful and rose to be a queen. And your fame spread among the nations on account of your beauty, because the splendor I had given you made your beauty perfect, declares the Sovereign Lord (Ezekiel 16:8-14).

You have been called and appointed to live *"for such a time as this"* (Esther 4:14). Now I know that many Christians have thrown that Scripture passage around so that it has become somewhat cliché, but I want to direct your gaze to the preceding words in the same sentence. These words are seldom quoted; they say, *"And who knows but that **you have come to a royal position for such a time as this"*** (Esther 4:14). Jesus is the King of kings, and we are joint heirs with Him when we have the Holy Spirit (see

Rev. 17:14). So we have come into a royal position because we are joint heirs with Jesus Christ (see Rom. 8:17).

We read that Esther spent six months with the oils and six months with perfumes and cosmetics (see Esther 2:12). Symbolically, the oil is the Holy Spirit. When the Lord comes to me, sometimes I smell floral fragrances and perfumes. Esther is a metaphor for someone who spends time in the presence of God. When we are immersed in the Holy Spirit, we begin to be elevated by the Holy Spirit in authority and in power. We begin to draw on our royal position, and we can command sickness and demons to go, and righteousness to come and manifest. Do you want to come to a royal position *"for such a time as this?"* This is the call to the Church in this hour—for all of us to come into our royal positions in Jesus Christ.

TRANSFORMING OUR TIME

Paul tells us that *"The Spirit Himself testifies with our spirit that we are God's children. Now if we are children, then we are heirs—heirs of God and co-heirs with Christ..."* (Rom. 8:16-17). If we are filled with the Holy Spirit and He testifies we are children of God and co-heirs with Christ, then since Jesus Christ is the King of kings, we may *"have come to a royal position for such a time as this."* We are called in Genesis to have dominion over creation: *"Let Us make man in Our image, in Our likeness, and let them rule..."* and human beings were made *"...in the image of God..."* (Gen. 1:26-27). And God blessed them and told them to be fruitful and multiply, and Adam was told to subdue and *"rule over"* the earth and all the animals (see Gen. 1:28).

In Chapter Five, I discussed how Jesus was clothed with a brilliant white light and how it is likely that Adam and Eve were also initially clothed with a brilliant white light—the glory of God which surrounded them when they were without sin. We are called to rule and subdue the earth as co-heirs with Christ, just as Adam and Eve were supposed to. So we step into our royal positions in Jesus Christ and wear the Designer's clothes just like Adam and Eve wore them before the fall.

In Ezekiel 16, the Lord speaks to His saints, telling us:

> *I spread the corner of My garment over you and covered your na-kedness. I gave you a solemn oath and entered into a covenant with you… I bathed you with water and washed the blood from you and put ointments on you* (Ezekiel 16:8-9).

Ointments are made of oil, so the water and the ointment from this Scripture are symbolic of the Holy Spirit. This passage in Ezekiel continues, *"And your fame spread among the nations on account of your beauty, because the splendor I had given you made your beauty perfect, declares the Sovereign Lord"* (Ezek. 16:14). These themes of being filled with the oils, being made beautiful, and fame being spread to the nations sound like being clothed in the Designer's clothes. The only difference is that the aim is to spread to the nations the Gospel of the Kingdom to testify about Jesus Christ and make Him famous in all the nations. God clearly wants to cover His people to make them beautiful lights that shine brightly for Him so they are able to transform the nations of the world for His name's sake.

We are blessed to be born at a time like this. No other generation has lived on the earth with so many people alive as there are today. There are more people alive today on earth than at any other time in the history of the world. This sets the stage for the global harvest. As a member of the army of God, filled with faith, you can make a significant eternal difference and have a lot of fun while doing it. If you get filled by the Holy Spirit and wear the Designer's clothes, you will be invited into a number of roles that believers can participate in, like the following:

- You are alive today and you are invited to become part of the army of God that is going to conquer the devil and his powers in the world.

- You are alive today and can become one of the saints who will possess the Kingdom of God as Daniel prophesied.

- You are alive today and can become a son of God who will liberate the creation from its bondages.

- You are alive today and can become a champion for God's Kingdom who will represent Jesus Christ on the earth and bring His Kingdom power to the people to heal them and the creation around the world.

- You are alive today to walk into your birthright that Jesus Christ planned for your life.

- You are alive today to participate in bringing in the largest harvest of souls in history, bringing Jesus fame as you go to the nations.

It is an exciting decision—will we move out in faith, hungering and thirsting to join the Kingdom exploits that will transform society because we are filled with the Holy Spirit? Or will we keep with the status quo church and remain hidden within the cultural landscape of the secular world? The choice is yours. However, I believe that this is a *kairos* time, a special season created by God for His Church body to grab hold of the Designer's clothes and put them on every single day until the wedding banquet.

POWER IMPACT

When the woman with the issue of blood came up to Jesus and touched His garment, she was immediately healed. *"At once Jesus realized that power had gone out from Him...*" (Mark 5:30). Jesus was the Son of God, and He had power going out from Him. When the sons of God appear on earth, they will also have power coming out from them. I am contending for that power, for *"... the Kingdom of Heaven has been forcefully advancing, and forceful men lay hold of it"* (Matt. 11:12). I am contending to lay hold of the Kingdom of Heaven, so I become all that God has destined for me to become.

I challenge you, the reader, to join me and pursue your birthright in Jesus Christ in this hour. I am not in a better position to grab hold of my birthright than anyone else is to grab theirs. But I am really hungry and thirsty for more of the Kingdom of God and more of Jesus. Faith, hunger, and thirst are currencies of Heaven. God is pleased when His children yearn for the Kingdom realities, yearn for what He desires to give us, and yearn for what He knows we need for this end-time hour.

- Will you join me and thirst for more of the Kingdom of Heaven?

- Will you be willing to surrender your life completely for Christ's sake?

- Are you willing to be a light and shine it brightly in the world around you?

- Are you willing to put on the Designer's clothes, or will you be satisfied wearing designer clothes?

- You were born to come to *a royal position for such a time as this.* So will you take the time to put on your royal robe—the Designer's clothes?

The implication of wearing the Designer's clothes is that you are wearing Jesus Christ, which means you will walk out in your birthright that God planned for you at this time in your life. When you wear the Designer's clothes, you will feel at home and know you were made to walk out demonstrating the Kingdom of God everywhere you go, bringing joy and glory to the Lord Jesus Christ. If you do not wear the Designer's clothes you might not make it into the wedding banquet, especially if you are living as the last generation on earth. Our lovely Lord has given us free will, so you can choose something else with which to occupy your life, but nothing else will be as rewarding—both in this life and afterwards—as wearing the Designer's clothes and walking out your royal position for such a time as this. I hope you will sincerely pray about the choice you are going to make.

~

Discussion Questions

1. Discuss your dream to become all that God intended you to become.

   ◦ How would you like to transform society?

   ◦ How would you like to see the gifts of the Holy Spirit demonstrated?

   ◦ How would you like to see the fruit of the Holy Spirit demonstrated?

   ◦ Pray for one another, blessing each other to walk out your dreams.

2. How have you come to a royal position at such a time as this?

   ◦ Discuss how you would walk out being a co-heir with Christ.

   ◦ Paul says, *"And God raised us up with Christ and seated us with Him in the heavenly realms…"* (Eph. 2:6). Discuss if we are seated with Christ.

   ◦ Christ *is* the King of kings. Does this give us a royal position or not?

3. Now that you have seen the implications of wearing the Designer's clothes, what are you feeling in your heart you will do?

   ◦ How will you go about doing this?

- What about hindrances and cultural pressures that will come against you? What will you do about them?

- What do you think about the implications of wearing or not wearing the Designer's clothes?

PRAYER

Are you willing to join me to become a wise virgin, a son of God, and to demonstrate Jesus everywhere you go by wearing the Designer's clothes? If so, pray this prayer out loud:

Heavenly Father, I thank You for Lord Jesus Christ and for all that He did for me. He saved me; by His stripes my body has been healed, His Holy Spirit fills me, making me a child of God, and He empowers me and will overshadow me. He also gave me every spiritual blessing in the heavenly realms, and I am allowed to become a co-heir with Jesus Christ so I can come to my royal position for a time like this.

I choose to die now, to lose my life—my will, my mind, and my emotions, and to take up life in You, Jesus.

Father, I ask for the grace to walk out my birthright in Christ. Please give me grace to come to You, to wait, and to receive the Holy Spirit. I ask for the grace to do this regularly. Then, Jesus, You will be living in me, and the overflow of the Holy Spirit will overshadow me so I will be in living in Jesus too.

Father, please give me boldness to step out into the calling You have on my life. I want to be one of Your bright lights in the world and to manifest Your Kingdom powers. I want to make

Jesus famous, so give me that boldness and the power to do all You have called me to do.

Blessings and glory and power to Your name, Lord Jesus Christ. Amen.

Epilogue

I received a prophecy in 2007 that said I would be "given the fires of God for evangelism," and I am now living in Seattle, Washington. To my joy, I discovered it is one of the lowest-churched regions in the United States. The fire has gotten much hotter in my hands these last few months. I used to tell the Brazilians that I felt 10 volts of power in my hands when I was in North America, but I felt 220 volts in Brazil. However, in Seattle, the fire is more powerful than the 220 volts I felt in Brazil. I now see people that I meet here in Seattle regularly encountering the Kingdom of God due to my wearing the Designer's clothes.

My Dream

On March 20, 2008, I had a dream, and I believe it was from God. In it, I was walking with another Christian man in a park that felt like Stanley Park in Vancouver, British Columbia, a park with ascending and descending hills. We walked up a trail, and suddenly a large gush of water about two meters high came forth and flooded everything. We struggled to stay dry and on our feet. After a while, another large gush of water came and flooded everywhere. At the top of the hill, we met some other Christians who were in our party, and someone said, "One area is a bit nasty down there. There's lots of gay sex and solicitation in that area."

Then another person came up from that area and told us, "The water cleared away all the filth. We walked down there, and water was flowing all over the ground." The dream ended.

The outpouring of the Spirit in Lakeland, Florida, began April 2, 2008. However, I did not sense that the dream was about Lakeland, although it could be connected. I thought the Lord was saying to me personally that a great outpouring will occur where I am living. I will be soaked and saturated in it, and I will bring people in ungodly lifestyles into the Kingdom of God, and I will see them transformed. I also sensed it was not just me who would be in it, but all who choose to receive the outpouring.

I can hardly wait for the increased outpouring for the Kingdom of God because it is already lots of fun to release it these days.

ENCOUNTERS

In April 2008, I flew home to Seattle from Los Angeles, and I was in the middle seat in my row. I felt as if I was overshadowed by the presence of God. It felt so heavy that I asked the woman next to me, "Do you feel anything unusual in the atmosphere of our row?" She did not feel anything different. I tried to impart to her, but she did not feel the Holy Spirit in her hands. I mentioned that I had witnessed a lot of healing and miracles since I was filled with the Holy Spirit. She asked if I could pray for her sore neck. I agreed and prayed for five minutes in Jesus' name, and she was healed. Then I tried to impart again, and she felt the Spirit this time. She was still skeptical, so I said, "OK, I will ask the Lord for a word of knowledge." I prayed in tongues silently for a minute, then I got a vision of her on a bicycle, and a man was with her on another bicycle. I told her about the vision and asked, "Is it relevant?"

She said, "Yes, my husband and I often go out on weekend bike trips for exercise."

She began to warm up to me, and she talked about her travels to Asia and going into a Buddhist temple. Then I sensed she had picked up an evil spiritual presence, and I suggested that she allow me to drive it away. She was Roman Catholic, but the impartation had not stayed in her hand, so I just asked her to pray with me first, and I led her in a sinner's prayer. Then I moved my hands up from her stomach to her head and commanded that ungodly spirit to leave.

She felt it come off her head, and she said she felt lighter afterwards. In the terminal at the baggage carousel she brought her friend over, and with a big smile she introduced her friend to me. I guess she had as much fun as I did. It was great to see the Lord's work during a two-hour flight that resulted in a healing, a word of knowledge, discerning an evil spirit, leading someone to be born again, driving out the evil spirit, and imparting the gifts of the Spirit. It is so much fun serving the Lord Jesus Christ; I love wearing the Designer's clothes.

I noticed that my waitress in a Seattle restaurant where I was eating had a symbol on her right forearm, so I asked her, "What is that?" She said it was a Hindu symbol. I asked, "Is that the spiritual path you are following?"

"No," she replied, "I am more Buddhist."

"Oh, the person sitting across from me recently received freedom from a Buddhist spirit," I said.

Then I asked her to point her fingers to my fingers, and she felt the anointing and said, "That's the Chi."

I replied, "No, this is the Holy Spirit, and His power started flowing out of me after I invited Him to fill me over several months, and now I pray for sick people in Jesus' name, and they get healed." Then I said, "The anointing is going up your arm and into your body."

And she replied with a strained look on her face, "Yes, it is; that's all very interesting."

I immediately sensed her stomach was upset. I realized that it probably was a demon being disturbed by the Holy Spirit coming into her body. She walked away. After serving us the meal and clearing away our plates, I had the opportunity to ask her, "When you were feeling the Holy Spirit coming from me and entering your body earlier, I sensed your stomach was upset. Was I accurate with what I was sensing?"

She said, "Yes, I felt nauseous."

I replied, "I suggest you read the New Testament again and look where Jesus healed people by casting out evil spirits, because I think an evil spirit was in your stomach and was reacting to the Holy Spirit, and that caused your nausea."

She had alluded to me earlier that she was formerly a Christian, and she thanked me for my suggestion. I felt completely satisfied when I completed the task that the Lord had appointed for me to do with the waitress that night. I am pleased to be serving the Lord in all of the spontaneous encounters He brings to me, as they are both rewarding and fun.

When I was at FedEx Kinko's, an employee was watching me look at my hands. I had noticed earlier when I was at church that my hands were covered in glory dust. The guy asked me, "Did you hurt your hands?"

"No," I said, "I was just looking for the glory dust on my hands, but it's gone now." He looked amused, so I asked him if he could feel the anointing flowing out of my hands. He did, and the female employee who was standing there said she wanted to feel it, too.

When she did she said, "I read a book and everyone has that." But I explained it came from having soaked in the Holy Spirit for months, and then the Spirit began to flow out of me, and I started seeing healings happen in Jesus' name. I told her she was very sensitive to the spiritual realm, and I asked her if she had any spiritual beliefs. She told me she was agnostic. Just then I discerned there was an angel present, so I told her, "Come over here and see if you can feel this angel." She came to my side of the counter, and I said to her, "Move your hand slowly through the air and see if you can feel the power change."

She felt both sides of the angel and then said, "What is he doing here?"

I said, "He is here to help me demonstrate the Kingdom of God and tell you who Jesus is."

These evangelistic encounters occur regularly for me now. The key is that I have been filled with the Holy Spirit continually, and I am now wearing the Designer's clothes. Wearing them enables me to demonstrate the Kingdom of God and tell the people that Jesus is the King of kings everywhere I go.

There is a great harvest in the world today. More people are alive today than there have ever been alive at one time. In Matthew 10, Jesus *"called the disciples to Him and gave them authority to drive out evil spirits, and to heal every disease and sickness"* (Matt. 10:1). Why? It was because in the previous chapter of Matthew, Jesus said to the disciples, *"The harvest is plentiful but the workers are few. Ask the Lord of the harvest, therefore, to send out workers into His harvest field"* (Matt. 9:37-38). The Lord of the harvest wants to empower the disciples with the authority and power in Jesus' name to drive out demons, heal the sick, and proclaim that the

Kingdom of Heaven is near. That's what I am called to do, and I get so much joy and satisfaction from releasing the Kingdom of God and seeing people being brought closer to know Jesus.

I recently put together a training module called Kingdom Evangelism, which involves the following:

1. Being filled with the Holy Spirit

2. Prophecy and words of knowledge

3. Healing the sick

4. Binding evil spirits and deliverance from demons

5. Kingdom evangelism—putting it all together and preaching the Gospel

All of the above operations of the Holy Spirit have occurred in my life only because I asked and waited for the Holy Spirit to fill me and clothe me in *The Designer's clothes*. My next book project comes from this training module and will be called: *Surprisingly Supernatural: A Practical Guide to Releasing the Gifts of the Spirit.*

I had an invitation to travel to Sao Paulo, Brazil, and I ended up sharing in seven churches. The response was very good, and I now have invitations from nine churches for my next trip to Brazil. God took me to a higher level on this trip. I prophesied to many people and had a national prophecy for Brazilians that I was told other prophets had also given. I was encouraged, as I had not heard the messages from other people or prophets, so I knew I had heard from God. I saw four people with eye problems all miraculously healed, and I drove demons out of other people. The Lord also helped me to encourage other believers on this trip to step out in faith and get filled by the Spirit, to lay hands on people to heal the sick, to drive out demons, and to speak forth prophetic words. The

Lord also gave me discernment for angels, orbs, and spiritual knives in believer's backs.

I shake my head in wonder at how much my life has now changed, for five years ago none of this was opened to me, but now that I am being possessed by the Holy Spirit and transformed from glory to glory, I see the Kingdom being released every day of my life. I love releasing the Kingdom of God, and I can only do that because He has clothed me in the Designer's clothes. I will fast and pray to hear the next step as to where the Lord wants to take me in my birthright, which likely will include conducting Kingdom Evangelism workshops locally and also taking some mission trips overseas.

God is so good and His love endures forever, and I am so excited to operate in my Father's Kingdom and to see what is the next exciting and adventurous activity He will allow me to participate in. I hope you can join me in the joy and fun of being God's children who bring His Kingdom into the lives of the people around us. Be blessed, and be a blessing—be filled with the Holy Spirit, be transformed by the power of God, and put on the Designer's clothes.

Blessings,
Neil J. Gilligan DPM, MPM, MCS

Appendix A

Soaking

"Soaking" is the term used to describe allowing yourself to bask in the river of God, which is the presence of God. This is what I do when I soak: I lay down on the floor with my face up, but I can also do it while sitting as well. I open my hands with the palms facing the ceiling. I begin by putting on instrumental worship music that is soft and draws my heart into intimacy with God. I position my mind and emotions to relax and be at peace. This preparation is to cause my faith to rise, so that I express my desire to spend time with my Father and my Lord Jesus and to be filled by the Holy Spirit.

I invite God to fill me with His Spirit, because Isaiah says if we are thirsty we can come to the waters and drink (see Isa. 55:1). I ask God to fill me with His Spirit, displaying my thirst and desire for Him and His will, for I understand, "'... *Not by might nor by power, but by My Spirit,' says the Lord Almighty*" (Zech. 4:6). Therefore, I am dependant on the Holy Spirit to empower me and guide me into everything that the Lord has for me. I continue soaking by asking the Holy Spirit, the Spirit of Truth, and the seven Spirits of God to fill me. I also declare Scriptures that impacted the first disciples of Jesus Christ, and I tell the Father in Heaven that I want to receive the blessing of His Holy Spirit.

I may vary what I say on different days, but this is an example of a fuller expression of how I ask God to fill me:

> *Heavenly Father, I ask You to send Your Holy Spirit and fill me, because Your Word tells me:*

- *"'... Not by might nor by power, but by My Spirit,' says the Lord Almighty"* (Zech. 4:6). Lord, I believe it is only by Your Spirit, so please fill me with Your Spirit.

- *"... Be filled with the Spirit"* (Eph. 5:18). Lord, let me be continually filled by your Holy Spirit.

- Jesus, You said to Your first disciples, *"As the Father has sent Me, I am sending you,"* and then You breathed on them and said, *"receive the Holy Spirit"* (John 20:21-22). Lord, breathe on me, and send me. I want to go out like You were sent out. Let me receive Your Holy Spirit.

- And Jesus, You said, *"... How much more will your Father in Heaven give the Holy Spirit to those who ask Him"* (Luke 11:13). Father in Heaven, I ask for You to please fill me with Your Holy Spirit.

- Paul tells us that the Holy Spirit will sanctify Gentiles like me (see Rom. 15:16). Holy Spirit, please come and fill me and sanctify me and make me holy.

- And Jesus, You said that if a man remains in You, and You remain in Him, then he will bear much fruit, but without You he can do nothing (see John 15:5). I believe that, Lord, so please remain in me and fill me with Your Spirit.

- Holy Spirit of God, please come and fill me now; come Counselor, come Spirit of Truth, teach me—teach me all things and guide me into all truth (see John 14:25; 16:13).

Revelation speaks about the seven Spirits of God and says that the seven Spirits of God who are before the throne of God are the seven eyes of the Lamb (see Rev. 4:5; 5:6). And Isaiah 11:2 gives the names of the seven Spirits of God, which are the following:

- The Spirit of the Lord

- The Spirit of wisdom

- The Spirit of understanding (revelation)

- The Spirit of counsel

- The Spirit of power

- The Spirit of knowledge

- The Spirit of the fear of the Lord

I also often say, "Spirit of the Lord, please come and fill me, teach me, guide me, and be with me all day long. Spirit of wisdom, please come and fill me, teach me, guide me, and be with me all day long." And I continue to invite each of the seven Spirits of God to fill me.

I understand that it is, *"Not by might nor by power, but by My Spirit,"* says the Lord (Zech. 4:6). So I am dependant on the Holy Spirit to empower me and guide me into everything that the Lord has for me.

After I invite the Holy Spirit and the seven Spirits of God to fill me, I wait expectantly for Him. I focus my mind and heart on Jesus, and my attitude is to have more of Him. I want to know Him more. I spend as much time as I can in God's presence. I do it in the morning when I awake, at night before I go to sleep, and in the car—just everywhere I can.

I also do it continually, meaning each and every day. I have spent too much of my life trying to be equipped in human ways to do God's work, but now I understand that all those ways are bankrupt. I just need more of Jesus, and then I am able to release more of His Kingdom around me.

Now I encourage you to invite the Holy Spirit to come and fill you and then wait for Him and engage with the Lord, for *"God is Spirit, and His worshippers must worship in spirit and in truth"* (John 4:24).

APPENDIX B

SCRIPTURE REFERENCES TO BEING CLOTHED

In Romans 13, Paul teaches along the end-time theme I have pointed out in this book, for he says:

And do this, understanding the present time. The hour has come for you to wake up from your slumber, because our salvation is nearer now than when we first believed. The night is nearly over; the day is almost here. So let us put aside the deeds of darkness and put on the armor of light. Let us behave decently, as in the daytime... clothe yourselves with the Lord Jesus Christ, and do not think about how to gratify the desires of the sinful nature (Romans 13:11-14).

He also says in Galatians:

You are all Sons of God through faith in Christ Jesus, for all of you who were baptized into Christ have clothed yourselves with Christ (Galatians 3:26-27).

Paul points out in these two verses that we need to wake up, as the endtimes are near. So we need to put on the armor of light and clothe ourselves with the Lord Jesus Christ. This is the same thing I am saying here in this book—wake up, put on the Designer's clothes, and live a life worthy of the calling by loving the Lord, by being with Him, by Him being in you, and by you being in Him (see John 14:20). This especially helps you in testifying that Jesus Christ is alive and working through you by the performance of the spiritual gifts and the love you exude.

Paul also writes:

> *In reading this, then, you will be able to understand my insight into the mystery of Christ, which was not made known to men in other generations as it has now been revealed by the Spirit to God's holy apostles and prophets* (Ephesians 3:4-5).

So I humbly suggest that the purpose of this book and this appendix is to help bring the mystery of Christ to the present generations of believers. To further help you, below are a variety of other Scriptures that refer either directly or indirectly to being clothed in Christ; however, this is not an exhaustive list.

Being Clothed

> *The man and his wife were both naked, and they felt no shame* (Genesis 2:25).

> *... he ate it. Then the eyes of both of them were opened, and they realized they were naked* (Genesis 3:6-7).

> *Awake, awake, O Zion, clothe yourself with strength. Put on your garments of splendor...* (Isaiah 52:1).

I delight greatly in the Lord; my soul rejoices in my God. For he has clothed me with garments of salvation and arrayed me in a robe of righteousness... (Isaiah 61:10).

Remain in Me, and I will remain in you. No branch can bear fruit by itself; it must remain in the Vine. Neither can you bear fruit unless you remain in Me (John 15:4).

On that day you will realize that I am in My Father, and you are in Me, and I am in you (John 14:20).

Now the Lord is the Spirit, and where the Spirit of the Lord is, there is freedom. And we, who with unveiled faces all reflect the Lord's glory, are being transformed into His likeness with ever-increasing glory, which comes from the Lord, who is the Spirit (2 Corinthians 3:17-18).

Meanwhile we groan, longing to be clothed with our Heavenly dwelling, because when we are clothed, we will not be found naked. For while we are in this tent, we groan and are burdened, because we do not wish to be unclothed but to be clothed with our heavenly dwelling, so that what is mortal may be swallowed up by life. Now it is God who has made us for this very purpose and has given us the Spirit as a deposit, guaranteeing what is to come (2 Corinthians 5:2-5).

But everything exposed by the light becomes visible, for it is light that makes everything visible. This is why it is said: "Wake up, O sleeper, rise from the dead, and Christ will shine on you."... But understand what the Lord's will is.... Be filled with the Spirit (Ephesians 5:13-14,17-18).

Behold, I come like a thief! Blessed is he who stays awake and keeps his clothes with him, so that he may not go naked and be shamefully exposed (Revelation 16:15).

Therefore, as God's chosen people, holy and dearly loved, clothe yourselves with compassion, kindness, humility, gentleness and patience (Colossians 3:12).

... You may participate in the divine nature and escape the corruption in the world caused by evil desires (2 Peter 1:4).

If we walk in the light, as He is in the light, we have fellowship with one another, and the blood of Jesus, His Son, purifies us from all sin (1 John 1:7).

No one who lives in Him keeps on sinning... (1 John 3:6).

Rather, clothe yourselves with the Lord Jesus Christ, and do not think about how to gratify the desires of the sinful nature (Romans 13:14).

For those God foreknew He also predestined to be conformed to the likeness of His Son, that He might be the firstborn among many brothers (Romans 8:29).

While they were wondering about this, suddenly two men in clothes that gleamed like lightening stood beside them (Luke 24:4).

I am going to send you what My Father has promised; but stay in the city until you have been clothed with power from on high (Luke 24:49).

... Jesus stood and said in a loud voice, "If anyone is thirsty, let him come to Me and drink. Whoever believes in Me, as the Scripture

has said, streams of living water will flow from within him" (John 7:37-38).

Put on the full armor of God... the belt of truth... the breastplate of righteousness... feet fitted with the gospel of peace... the shield of faith... the helmet of salvation and the sword of the Spirit (Ephesians 6:13-17).

For all of you who were baptized into Christ have clothed yourselves with Christ (Galatians 3:27).

... So let us put aside the deeds of darkness and put on the armor of light (Romans 13:12).

... For the trumpet will sound, the dead will be raised imperishable, and we will be changed. For the perishable must clothe itself with the imperishable and the mortal with immortality (1 Corinthians 15:52-53).

To [the saints] God has chosen to make known among the Gentiles the glorious riches of... the hope of glory. ... To this end I labor, struggling with all His energy, which so powerfully works in me (Colossians 1:27,29).

In Him and through faith in Him we may approach God with freedom and confidence (Ephesians 3:12).

Set your minds on things above, not on earthly things. For you died, and your life is now hidden with Christ in God. When Christ, who is your life, appears, then you also will appear with Him in glory (Colossians 3:2-4).

... be holy, because I am Holy (Leviticus 11:44).

But solid food is for the mature, who by constant use have trained themselves to distinguish good from evil (Hebrews 5:14).

…You may participate in the divine nature and escape the corruption of the world caused by evil desires (2 Peter 1:4).

… His clothes became white as the light (Matthew 17:2).

Sanctification

Now I commit you to God and to the word of His grace, which can build you up and give you an inheritance among all those who are sanctified (Acts 20:32).

To be a minister of Christ Jesus to the Gentiles with the priestly duty of proclaiming the gospel of God, so that the Gentiles might become an offering acceptable to God, sanctified by the Holy Spirit (Romans 15:16).

And that is what some of you were. But you were washed, you were sanctified, you were justified in the name of the Lord Jesus Christ and by the Spirit of our God (1 Corinthians 6:11).

For the unbelieving husband has been sanctified through his wife, and the unbelieving wife has been sanctified through her believing husband. Otherwise your children would be unclean, but as it is, they are holy (1 Corinthians 7:14).

How much more severely do you think a man deserves to be punished who has trampled the Son of God under foot, who has treated as an unholy thing the blood of the covenant that sanctified him, and who has insulted the Spirit of grace? (Hebrews 10:29)

May God Himself, the God of peace, sanctify you through and through. May your whole spirit, soul and body be kept blameless at the coming of our Lord Jesus Christ (1 Thessalonians 5:23).

But we ought always to thank God for you, brothers loved by the Lord, because from the beginning God chose you to be saved through the sanctifying work of the Spirit and through belief in the truth (2 Thessalonians 2:13).

TRANSFORMATION

…Who, by the power that enables Him to bring everything under His control, will transform our lowly bodies so that they will be like His glorious body (Philippians 3:21).

Do not conform any longer to the pattern of this world, but be transformed by the renewing of your mind… (Romans 12:2).

… May your priests, O Lord God, be clothed with salvation… (2 Chronicles 6:41).

We proclaim Him, admonishing and teaching everyone with all wisdom, so that we may present everyone perfect in Christ. To this end I labor, struggling with all His energy, which so powerfully works in me (Colossians 1:28-29).

You say, "I am rich; I have acquired wealth and do not need a thing." But you do not realize that you are… naked (Revelation 3:17).

Behold, I come like a thief! Blessed is he who stays awake and keeps his clothes with him, so that he may not go naked and be shamefully exposed (Revelation 16:15).

At that time the Kingdom of Heaven will be like ten virgins... (Matthew 25:1).

"Friend," He asked *"how did you get in here without wedding clothes?"* (Matthew 22:12)

If that is how God clothes the grass of the field, which is here today and tomorrow is thrown into the fire, will He not much more clothe you, O you of little faith? (Matthew 6:30).

Appendix C

Testimonies

Neil just asked me to do an experiment with him. We stood a couple of feet apart with his "fire" or energy that gives him God's healing powers, and he extended that to me, or toward me. I could feel the tingling in my fingers that were outstretched in his direction. We slowly moved apart and even after almost 60 feet I still felt the "fire." As he spoke in tongues, I could not stop my fingers from moving. But mostly, I felt so energized and I am still tingling all over my body and feel almost intoxicated.

Cherie Glahn
Dec 5, 2007

I am writing this testimony about my meeting Neil Gilligan at a Christian International Conference this past September 2007 in Santa Rosa Beach, Florida. Neil attended the Prophetic Deliverance class with Bob and Sharon Parkes with me and forty other class members. Neil had been one of the team members who assisted with my personal deliverance. I was seated on a chair while half a dozen class members were calling out the names of spirits that they thought may have been harassing me. However, Neil did something in addition to calling out names of spirits. Neil pointed the fingers of his hands toward my torso, and said something like, "I command all ungodly spirits must leave now in the name of Jesus Christ. I command that you must come up and out on the breath now." Then he would move his fingers upward, with palms facing upwards, pointing the whole time toward my body—beginning in my abdomen area—and slowly moving them up toward my throat. As he moved his fingers, I felt as if he was scooping up the ungodly spirits and forcing them to come up, and when they reached my throat they just came out as I breathed out.

At one point, Sharon asked Neil and the other men to back away from me, as she explained that many other trauma victims with similar experiences as mine had become uncomfortable with men touching them or even being too close during deliverance. So Neil began to back away (along with the other men); however, I began to protest and declared that he was helping, for when he moved his hands up it felt as if he was scooping the demons out; I wanted him to continue. I felt considerable freedom from this session, and I want to thank Neil Gilligan for being a helpful servant of the Lord Jesus Christ, for he was a channel of Jesus' power which brought me to greater freedom. And of course I am forever thankful for Jesus Christ for saving my soul and bringing me into great freedom. Praise the Lord!

Blessings,
Jodi Byrns
October 18, 2007

We are writing this testimony about our meeting with Neil Gilligan, who came to stay with us in our apartment June 28 through July 18, 2007 in São Paulo, Brazil. The first night Neil was with us we went out to dinner at a local pizza restaurant. Neil sat next to Marcio, and Naura sat across the table from Marcio and diagonally across from Neil. After a while, Neil asked me, Naura, to point the fingers of my left hand toward his hand, which was pointing toward me from a distance of about twenty centimeters. Neil said, "I just want to see what will happen as the Holy Spirit is released, so let's just leave our hands like this for a while."

After a few seconds, I began to feel a tingling sensation in my fingertips, and some heat; then it gradually progressed into my fingers, then into the palm of my hand up my forearm, then up my bicep to my shoulders, and then up the left side of my neck where I had some pain from an injury. Neil did not say a word about what was happening; he just kept pointing his hand toward mine. Well, I began to feel the pain in my neck diminish; and then, suddenly, all the pain was gone and I was healed. I told Neil and my husband Marcio, "The Holy Spirit just healed my neck."

They looked a little surprised, and Neil smiled and said, "Well, God knew you had pain there and wanted to heal you."

We were really touched by Neil's visit; he brought us into a closer relationship with God and showed how He wants to move through all believers with healing, deliverance, and prophetic words.

Blessings,
Marcio and Naura
July 2007

To the best of my memory:

Neil came over to me and asked me if I could tell what was on his head in the spiritual realm. He was sensing a pressure all around his head. I put my hand up and didn't really feel anything, but had an immediate sense of a helmet such as a Roman soldier might have worn in biblical times. It would've had a piece that came down between the eyes and over the nose.

Blessings,
Barbara Parker

I believe we were ministering purpose and destiny, and I distinctly remember waiting for the Lord to give me a word regarding my brother in Christ. As I was waiting, I also remember feeling as though I was not receiving anything at the time, but as I was looking into his eyes and continued to wait, a vision of a flickering flame appeared in the iris (the colored area) of his eye. For a moment I continued to wait, because I was not sure if this was a thought from myself or from the Throne. I waited until this image reappeared, and I realized that although this made no sense to me, this is what I was supposed to minister about to my brother in Christ. As I began to share with him what I was seeing, it was as though the flame began to burn consistently, just like a flame on the top of a candle.

Antonio C. Perry, M.A.

Appendix D

Supernatural Training Information

The following is only a partial list of some of the supernatural training schools that help believers to move into the supernatural realms of faith and to demonstrate the Kingdom of God and show that Jesus Christ is the King of kings and the Lord of lords.

Dr. Bill Hamon's Christian International is renowned for its excellent training in the prophetic, and it also offers other training in deliverance, apostolic training, and worship. The website is www.christianinternational.org. Phone: (850) 231-2600.

Graham Cooke has a School of Prophecy with United Christian Ministries:

PO Box 91

Southampton SO15 5ZE, United Kingdom

Elijah House offers a prophetic school and training on inner healing and deliverance. For more information contact Lois Hochstatter by email or phone. eh.liveschools@gmail.com. Phone: (509) 321-1255.

Patricia King offers a Prophetic Boot Camp and prophetic evangelism. Contact her at www.extremeprophetic.com.

Randy Clark has schools of healing throughout North America, and he also has a supernatural school. Their website is www.globalawakening.com.

Dr. Paul Cox teaches workshops on discernment and generational deliverance. His website is www.ashlandsplace.com.

Neil Lozano and his wife, Janet, teach on deliverance, and their website is www.heartofthefather.com

Cal Pierce is the director of the Healing Rooms, and they have workshops on healing and other supernatural training in conferences or in training schools. Their website is www.healingrooms.com.

Francis and Judith MacNutt teach on healing and deliverance from evil spirits, and can be contacted at www.christianhealingmin.org.

There are many more supernatural training schools and courses providing training that I have not mentioned here.

Inner Healing References

Ellel Ministries

Ellel Grange, Sussex England

- Telephone: (0) 1 323 440440

- E-mail: info@glyndley.ellel.org.uk

Ellel Canada, Ontario

- Telephone: (905) 457-5047 ext. 23

- E-mail: ellelca@sympatico.ca

Elijah House Prayer Counseling

Telephone: (509) 321-1255
Fax: (509) 321-1250
Mail: Elijah House
317 N. Pines Road
Spokane Valley, WA 99206

Restoring the Foundations (RTF)

- Telephone: (828) 696-9075 ext. 522

- E-mail: resources@phw.org

- Fax: (206) 339-2904

  Mail: Proclaiming His Word Resources
  2849 Laurel Park Highway
  Hendersonville, NC 28739

Some other names of Inner Healing Ministries are:

The Healing Rooms, Spokane, Washington
TACF prayer counseling, Toronto, Ontario
SOZO ministry, Bethel Church, Redding, California
Theophostic Prayer Ministry, phone: (270) 465-3757

ABOUT THE AUTHOR

Neil J. Gilligan, DPM (Doctorate of Practical Ministry), MCS (Master of Christian Studies), MPM (Master of Practical Ministry), was a trainer and the contact person with the International Association of Healing Rooms out of Spokane, Washington. He has traveled on nine short-term mission trips with private mission groups to Asia, Central America, and South America, and he has also traveled with Global Awakening. His book, *Transformed by the Power of God,* emerged from these previous experiences.

Neil ministers in evangelism, prophecy, healing, discernment, deliverance, and teaching. He is an equipper and trainer of the Body of Christ and has a call to the nations to bring the Gospel of Jesus Christ. He currently lives in Bellevue, Washington, and works with and is accountable to Open Heart Ministry and Bethesda Fellowship where Neil ministers as the team leader for evangelism. Neil is available for speaking engagements and training and equipping seminars that include topics such as healing the sick, deliverance, discernment, and evangelism training. The next book Neil is working on is called, *Surprisingly Supernatural: A Practical Guide to Releasing the Gifts of the Spirit,* which he hopes will be published in Spring of 2011. You may contact Neil Gilligan at surprisinglysupernatural@gmail.com or visit his website: www.flame-of-fire.com.

DESTINY IMAGE PUBLISHERS, INC.

*"Speaking to the Purposes of God for This Generation
and for the Generations to Come."*

VISIT OUR NEW SITE HOME AT
WWW.DESTINYIMAGE.COM

FREE SUBSCRIPTION TO DI NEWSLETTER

Receive free unpublished articles by top DI authors, exclusive
discounts, and free downloads from our best and newest books.

Visit www.destinyimage.com to subscribe.

Write to: Destiny Image
              P.O. Box 310
              Shippensburg, PA 17257-0310

Call: 1-800-722-6774

Email: orders@destinyimage.com

For a complete list of our titles or to place an order
online, visit www.destinyimage.com.